A
ROYAL COUPLING

THE HISTORIC MARRIAGE OF
BARNUM AND BAILEY

BY WILLIAM L. SLOUT

AN EMERITUS ENTERPRISE BOOK
SAN BERNARDINO, CALIFORNIA
2000

This book is dedicated to His Eminence
of early circus research and dear friend
STUART THAYER

CONTENTS

INTRODUCTION

1870, THE BEGINNING OF A NEW DECADE and a fresh start. Although the American circuses as a body held their own throughout the traumatic war years, they experienced periods of uncertainty, moments of danger, and frequent hardships from travel and living conditions. And, as a final farewell to the 1860s, 1869 was disastrous for them all. From the outset of that summer season and until time for returning to winter quarters, from spring until fall, they suffered under continual downpours of rain which created quagmires that made travel difficult and at times impossible, even for light vehicles. It has been estimated that out of some twenty or more well-known circus organizations that began the season only a mere half-dozen ended financially stable. Still, most of them returned to welcome in the 1870s and, in spite of the unfortunate previous season, looked toward to a promising future, an incentive that motivated the improvement and enlargement of their properties. Similar optimism encouraged new ownerships.

At that point in time such sanguinity was justified. The national audience was on the increase. Immigration accounted for a sizable influx of people who welcomed the sort of diversion circuses offered. Between 1860 and 1900 the population of the United States increased from 31 million to 76 million, with foreign arrivals accounting for 14 million of that total. Before 1880 the majority of aliens came from northern and Western Europe—the Scandinavian countries, England, Ireland, and Germany. With the exception of the Irish, who tended to settle in the already populated eastern states, most of the other nationalities migrated to the Middle West. Many were farmers who located in the expanses being opened for settlement as the western movement accelerated following the war. As a result, by 1870 the center of population was located at a point somewhere in south-central Ohio. This accounts for the clustering of circuses within those middle western states.

During the 1870s circuses experienced an expansion of territory. The South had opened up for travel following the cessation, which afforded many of the troupes a longer season. Rapid farm settlement in Wisconsin, Minnesota and points west created a growing number of agricultural and commercial centers, allowing circuses to attain more viable routes when traveling through those areas. The post-war cattle boom in Texas was an invitation for more shows to travel there. And the symbolic trans-continental tour of the Castello/Nixon circus of 1869, which went from coast to coast by rail and wagon, paved the way for others to make similar westward treks.

At various points during the decade each of the major circuses turned to rail as a permanent mode of transportation. Following 1865 there was a rash of war-torn railroad rebuilding in the South and a major effort to increase track mileage westward. By 1870 Southern roads were in surprisingly good condition. That same year there was an estimated total of 12,000 track miles west of the Mississippi River. Ten years later the figure had increased to 32,000. During these years spur lines were being added in all of the farm dominated states to facilitate getting the produce to centers of commerce. Texas greatly increased its usable rails in the 1870s from 711 to over 3,000 miles by 1880.

The new track mileage greatly affect the major circuses in two ways. It allowed them to make longer jumps to larger population centers, thereby passing up the smaller stands that rarely paid a profit but were necessary to break up a long move. And secondly, the shorter lines that fed into the large cities were used for excursion trains to transport audiences from those smaller places. The result, as we shall see, was that circuses could dramatically enlarge, both in seating accommodations and in arenic entertainment, and still find financial success.

James A. Bailey and P. T. Barnum joined forces to take out a double show for 1881—a royal coupling—inaugurating the "golden age" of the American circus. This book details some of the activity leading up to that notable landmark in amusement history. If it were a drama and circuses were characters in it, the playbook would list four of them. Taking the leading roles would be P. T. Barnum's Greatest Show on Earth and Cooper & Bailey's Great International, with the two other players being Howes' Great London and Adam Forepaugh's famous circus and menagerie. The scene of conflict would occur in the United States from 1871 through 1881. There would be, however, retrospective action that is important to the narrative going back several years, forming the roots of the drama, which we will examine when the curtain rises.

I am indebted to many people and organizations for supplying material used in this book. I would particularly like to acknowledge the Pfening Archives, Columbus, Ohio; Lee Bayer and Annie Hopkins at Inter-Library Loan, California State University Library, San Bernardino, California; and Fred Dahlinger, Jr., and staff at the Robert L. Parkinson Library and Research Center, Circus World Museum, Baraboo, Wisconsin, where most of the textual research and pictorial illustrations were acquired.

Some of the material for Part I, detailing the first three years of the Barnum show, was taken from Thayer's and Slout's *Grand Entrée: The Birth of the Greatest Show on Earth* (see bibliography). I am grateful to my co-author from that endeavor for allowing me to use it.

William L. Slout

"Oh, Mr. Bailey."

"Yes, Mr. B.?"

"Would you like to share a double show with me?
 You can rise to great acclaim
 If you but use that famous name."

"You mean 'Bailey,' Mr. Barnum?"

"Oh, no. 'Barnum,' Mr. B."

Phineas Taylor Barnum

PROLOGUE:
MR. BARNUM AND MR. BAILEY

ERHAPS THE MOST NOTEWORTHY EVENT in American circus history occurred in the year of 1871. It appeared when the magical name of P. T. Barnum was first prominently displayed on a circus bill, a name that was easily recognizable throughout not only the United States but in England and on the European continent.

Although Barnum had no such organization under his name before this year, in 1836, early in his career, he filled a brief engagement with Aaron Turner's circus as treasurer, secretary, and ticket seller. His only previous experience in show business had occurred the winter before when he exhibited the black woman Joice Heth, purported to have been the nurse of George Washington. Later, as his name became nationally recognized, he leased it out to various proprietors, but generally participated financially.

What may have been an exception was a concert troupe managed by Nichols, Totten & Co. It toured under the title of Barnum's Grand Traveling Exhibition in the summer of 1848. The only hint of a Barnum presence was the suggestion in the advertising that the program was "novel and entertaining, and at the same time instructive and free from the slightest objection from the moral and religious community," an amusement philosophy Barnum would espouse throughout his career. The tented attraction, under a 50 by 100 foot canvas, featured Billy Whitlock, the famous

banjoist and minstrel performer. Miss Emma Leslie was the
vocalist, and with a Mr. Hallif doubled in a comic skit called
"Yankee Courtship." The whole was concluded with the
playlet, "The Adventures and Mishaps of a Yankee Pedlar."

There was also a "busy city" (automated) representa-
tion of the funeral of Napoleon—"His removal from the Island of Helena, his reception in Paris, the whole funeral procession numbering over seven hundred thousand, and reach-
ing a distance of ten miles, with the magnificent Funeral Car,
drawn by sixteen horses, are all represented, not upon can-
vass but by moving figures, and so naturally do they move
along, keeping step with the solemn strain of the band of music, that the spectator almost imagines that he beholds real-
ity."[1] This automated spectacle may have been used as a
sideshow exhibit.

In 1851, Seth B. Howes, in partnership with Sherwood E. Stratton, organized the P. T. Barnum Asiatic Caravan, Museum and Menagerie. It was not a circus but a
tented organization that operated similar to one. The show
was an assortment of animals and oddities, General Tom
Thumb being the major attraction. There was an armless
man, a fat boy, wax representations of the United States
presidents, and sundry items from Barnum's museum in New
York. The menagerie consisted of nine elephants and some
caged animals under the supervision of Alviza Pierce, the
wild beast tamer. Although almost unanimously greeted by
the press as "the greatest humbug of the age," the show was
profitable throughout its four-year existence—the first two
under the management of Howes, the last two under L. B.
Lent.[2]

In 1855 the Barnum name appeared in Barnum and
Wood's Grand Baby Show. The toddler competition was
advertised for four days at New City Hall in Pittsburgh, with
prize money that amounted to $3,180—"Mr. Barnum will be

present and deliver the premiums in person." Other contests were held in Boston, Albany, and New York City.[3]

In 1860, Barnum joined with circus proprietor James M. Nixon to exhibit Grizzly Adams' California Menagerie under canvas at Broadway and Thirteenth Street, New York City (Barnum makes no mention of Nixon in his autobiography). The attraction opened on April 30 and continued until July 7; after which, Adams sold his share to Barnum, who then made a deal with Nixon to take the animals as part of Cooke's Royal Circus on tour through the New England states.

A show called the Barnum & Van Amburgh's Museum and Menagerie went out for the summer of 1867, with P. T. Barnum as its nominal president, Hyatt Frost as director, and Henry Barnum as manager. It consisted of the extensive stock of Van Amburgh animals, augmented by a number of curiosities from Barnum's museum. The exhibition was toured during the summer months and housed at the museum throughout the winter. Barnum claimed he owned forty percent of the enterprise, which was capitalized at a million dollars, and the Van Amburgh company had interest in the rest. "As one of the conditions of the new arrangement," Barnum stated in his autobiography, "it was stipulated that I should withdraw from all active personal attention to the Museum, but should permit my name to be announced as General Manager, and I was elected President of the company."[4] Here, as with the previous ventures, he was leasing his celebrity and influence to the management of others.

Dan Castello and W. C. Coup, who would become prominent members of the Barnum circus debut, organized a small Wisconsin show in 1870. They traveled by boat on the Great Lakes under the title of Dan Castello's Circus &

Egyptian Caravan. Castello was a clown and general performer and served as equestrian director; and Coup was in charge of the business end. The venture was successful in that the partners received added experience in show management, experience that would be applied to great effect in the next few years.

The property at the end of the season was valued by Coup at $30,000 and the summer, he stated, "was one of perpetual delight and not a little pecuniary profit." Then, the following year, these men, both from Wisconsin, provided the impetus for the first real circus upon which P. T. Barnum placed his name.

W. C. Coup, who as a youngster—he was fourteen—had worked on the 1852 P. T. Barnum Asiatic Caravan, Museum and Menagerie and must have observed the drawing power of the famous name, contacted Barnum in the fall of 1870 and offered him a percentage of the profits for its use. After Barnum refused, indicating no interest in getting back into show business, Coup wrote again, assuring him that all he wanted was an authorization to include "P. T. Barnum" within the title of his show. "Although his family and friends were opposed to the project, principally on account of his advanced age," Coup indicated later, "I, however, secured him as a partner, and this laid the foundation of the greatest amusement enterprise ever known in the history of the world."[5] Barnum's letter of acceptance was dated October 6, 1870. Included was a reference to a Cardiff giant that would not break, Siamese Twins, and other curiosities which Barnum suggested would be valuable features for the enterprise, an indication he was prepared to be involved with more than just his name.

Coup has stated that Barnum invested $100,000 in the project before he fully decided to go ahead with it. He also disclosed in an 1891 interview that the final decision came over a game of checkers in Barnum's office at the museum. The two were talking about the show when a bill writer by the name of Emerson interposed that he thought Barnum was a man of leisure.

"I thought so, too," Barnum replied as he jumped to his feet, spilling checkers over the office floor.

"Barnum," Coup interjected, "it's time to decide this thing now. You've got $100,000 in it. If you want to get out, all right."

"Well, I'm in it," Barnum said. "The checkers can lay where they are."[6]

In a letter to Moses Kimball dated February 18, 1871, Barnum wrote, "I thought I had finished the show business (and all others), but just for a flyer I go it once more."[7]

As indicated earlier, Coup's introduction to show business came when he joined Barnum's traveling museum and menagerie. Barnum did not tour with the show; and, even if he had, there is no reason to believe he would have known the young roustabout. Coup followed this by working with the L. G. Butler circus in some capacity. In the winter of 1860, he conducted a wax figure show in the Caribbean. The following year he joined the Mabie aggregation as manager of the sideshow with Harry Buckley, and continued through 1865, when he switched to Yankee Robinson's circus as sideshowman and an assistant to management. This was as close to actually operating a circus as he came before joining with Dan Castello in 1870.

Castello was the lesser partner in this new venture, which would be called P. T. Barnum's Great Traveling Museum, Menagerie, Caravan and Hippodrome. His circus career may have started in 1849, but it is not until 1854 that there is any reference to him. That is the year he moved to

William Cameron Coup

Delavan, Wisconsin, and there joined the Mabie Bros.' circus as an acrobat, most likely remaining with them through the 1855 season. The first announcement of his appearing as a clown came in 1856, when he was with the John Robinson show. The following year, he started out with Harry Buckley's National Circus, a Delavan company, but left in midseason to join Major Brown's, and in the winter performed for Spalding & Rogers in New Orleans. In 1858, he was connected with Satterlee, Bell & Co. as leaper and acrobat and the next year with James M. Nixon. By this time he had added animal training to his accomplishments with a bull named Don Juan that presumably performed such tricks as mounting pedestals, jumping hurdles, and the like.

He went to England in the fall of 1859, accompanied by the bull and a trained buffalo and was engaged with Hengler's circus, one of England's largest, but spent only part of 1860 touring with it. Toward the end of the summer he joined Howes & Cushing's American Circus in Ireland. After suffering injuries from an attack by the buffalo, and later while performing a leap, he returned to the United States in October of that year. He then appeared with Spalding & Rogers in New York for the winter season, and later aboard their *Floating Palace* in New Orleans.

In Fairplay, Wisconsin, in 1863, Castello and Richard VanValkenberg, a lead miner, organized Castello & Van-Vleck's Mammoth Circus for a season, which was fairly successful. The following year Dan Castello's Own Great Show chartered the steamboat *Jeannette Roberts*, and performed down the Mississippi and up and down the Ohio; then, in the fall, descended the Mississippi again to take advantage of the presence of the Union Army on the lower rivers. In 1865, Castello routed an upriver journey to Nashville, where he combined his show with one belonging to Seth B. Howes, managed by Howes' nephew, Egbert.

At the end of the year, Castello took James M. Nixon as a partner, buying the Howes' equipment and leasing some of its animals; and the two continued together for the next four years. Their final season of 1869 began with a route across the South to Savannah, from where they went north to Virginia and west to Tennessee, and then out to Kansas and Nebraska. They reached Omaha just as the Union Pacific Railroad was finishing its track to California. At Nixon's urging, the show was loaded onto railroad cars and proceeded across the plains to become the first circus in history to go coast to coast in a single season.

And now, in 1871, Coup and Castello were faced with an imposing challenge. As Stuart Thayer expressed it, they soon found out that Barnum was "in for a penny, in for a pound," when he enthusiastically set about lining up museum attractions for the new show. It wasn't just a circus Barnum had in mind; it was a complete amusement exhibition—a circus, a museum, and a menagerie, the largest ever attempted, all in a single package, all for a single admission price. It must have come as a shock to Coup and Castello. The two had taken a bold step into a partnership that had both advantages and disadvantages, most of which must have been quite obvious to them, men in their mid-thirties, casting their lot with a shrewd and experienced deal-maker of sixty. But could they handle a show of this immensity? Time would prove them worthy.

What was Barnum's working arrangement within this new management? The Barnum autobiography is of no help, the writing being too often unreliable and limited to self-deification. His knowledge of the circus business was limited. "As far as the technical details of the show were concerned," Coup said later, "Mr. Barnum was absolutely ignorant, but in its place he possessed an amount of commercial daring and business sagacity, that which amply atoned for his other shortcomings."[8]

Barnum himself admitted he knew nothing about the details of running a circus.[9] He had managed his museum and a few single attractions, but had arranged for surrogates to handle the day-to-day planning and on-the-job work in the other enterprises to which his name was connected.

His main interest was in acquiring and exhibiting oddities for the museum and animals for the menagerie. This was appropriate to his experience in and his knowledge of the amusement business. It was also indicative of his awareness of the public's sense of curiosity and their willingness to satisfy it by paying to see exotic things, animate and inanimate. And much to the distress of his partners, he spent huge sums of money building such collections.

Yet he showed no interest in circus performance. And, indeed, the word "circus" does not appear in the early show titles bearing his name. This has to be seen as a matter of financial shrewdness, because many people, morally opposed to circuses, willingly attended a P. T. Barnum show. And it perpetuated the image of piety Barnum had created for himself, perhaps in an attempt to compensate for his earlier depiction as a "humbug."

Tody Hamilton, long-time press agent for the Barnum show, made this observation:

> With the religious press Barnum passed as a model man; his show had earned, through their columns alone, the title of "Great Moral Show." This was encouraged by him with substantial patronage. He captured the temperance people with temperance speeches in the ring. At his residence in Bridgeport he created a sensation by emptying the contents of his wine cellar into the gutter with imposing demonstrations.[10]

As a business man Barnum has been described as shrewd, ingenious, far-seeing, adventurous, experimental, and observant of the demands of the public in the matter of amusements. Although big-hearted in giving away thousands to charities, he possessed a streak of parsimony which bordered on eccentricity. As one scribe characterized it, he was scrupulous in "getting every five-cent piece he thought he was entitled to, and, in spite of his open-handedness, he was as quick as lightning to see an opportunity to turn an honest penny."[11]

As the greatest promoter and advertiser of his day, he developed many devices that became established practice. A major contribution was his invention of the courier, a newspaper-type throwaway that was distributed ahead of the show to extol its wonders. In fact, the introduction of this type of advertising was the most important improvement in circus promotion since the advent of lithographed posters. Like the lithographs, the couriers were broadcast by the millions. He did much of the bill writing himself and attentively supervised the composition by others during the winter lay-off period.

But the greatest achievement resulting from his skills as a press agent was the "puffing" of his own image. No other man with national contributions so unimportant has received such attention and adoration from the American press and the American public. He contrived his own celebrity and bathed in it. His autobiography is an example of pure self-service and self-righteousness. And the thousands of copies of it sold from a circus highbox magnified the already self-made myth.

Agent John Dingess, in his unpublished manuscript, made these observations:

It is scarcely necessary to say that Mr. Barnum was subject to spells of inflation and egoism. He always wanted to be known as a wit, and his egoism, while it was not particularly offensive, oftentimes (sic) bordered upon the ridiculous. No man ever believed more firmly in his own greatness than Phineas Taylor Barnum. He felt that it was thrust upon him, and that he deserved no credit for achieving it, and no man ever lived who loved fame more than the bumptious old man, with his apparently harmless guile and sweet belief in his own incorruptible honesty.[12]

Throughout his career the print media appeared awed by his persona and indeed capitalized on his fame. But in spite of his apparent self-righteousness, the claims Barnum made in his advertisements, in his autobiography, and in his public statements were too often exaggerations or untruths.

One is hard-pressed to find public criticism of his professional activity from newspaper accounts or from personal associates. This writer was surprised at finding one such told to an *Ohio State Journal* reporter by Charles Stow,[13] who accused him of being "but the unsubstantial shadow of what the public took him for." Stow was an outstanding press agent during this period who worked for Barnum's organization from 1874 through 1877, and again in 1882, and was well acquainted with him. "No man is a hero to his valet," he stated, "and there is nothing heroic in Mr. Barnum to his intimate associates or employes." He continued:

He was the archetype of the shrewd, calculating, grasping Connecticut Yankee, enterprising without being liberal, a sharp, relentless bargainer, and one whose every undertaking centered in self.... In audacity of exaggeration he is unrivaled, and seemed even to prefer it when the truth would have answered as well.... His adulation of the press was as fulsome as it was empty. He was prodigal in praise but miserly in pay. While he was voicing grateful songs to the press as the creator and prime cause of his fortune, his agents were continually instructed to cut down advertising space, and the actual fact is that many shows whose receipts were not a tithe of his, and which scarcely received lines to his columns of notices, paid the newspapers more money than did his greatest show on earth.... Although practically he was a tyro in the circus business and could scarcely tell a rhinoceros from a tapir, his name was a tremendous magnet and drew out of all proportions to the merits of what it stood for.

Louis E. Cooke, another prominent press agent of the era, wrote that Barnum was not a practical circus man or promoter of big shows in the sense and degree of such circus proprietors as Adam Forepaugh, John Robinson, Seth B. Howes, Lewis B. Lent, and some others. "Still," he predicted, "the name of Barnum will unquestionably stand as a monument among and above all other men in the arenic world long after the most of them, who built up and shouldered the responsibilities of his enterprise, have been lost in tradition."[14]

However, it cannot be denied that as a showman he always gave the public more for their money than any one else, and he had the faculty of surrounding himself with men who could and did carry out his ideas to perfection without troubling him with the details. He was a silent partner in various amusement enterprises, always willing to take a good percentage of the receipts or profits; but if a loss or disaster occurred he was usually in a position to declare himself irresponsible.[15]

From 1871 until his death, Barnum did not travel with the designated P. T. Barnum shows. Rather, he would visit them for two or three days several times a year. Whenever that occurred the managers advertised it as a special attraction and the attendance increased. He rode around the track in his carriage during the performance, enjoying the applause, and then delivered a brief address. C. G. Sturtevant suggested that Barnum's greatest interest on these occasions was the number of copies of his autobiography that had been sold. He was a greater curiosity than any within his museum. Story has it that he once heard a small boy ask his father, "Say, pa, which cage is Barnum in?"[16] Indeed, the specter of him traveled with the shows under his name. Even in his absence his presence was felt. The press referred to him as if he were on the lot. The audiences came every day expecting to see him.

His public claims emphasized unique moral and educational values exhibited under his canvases and on giving the public more for the money than any other amusement organization. The latter was quite true. As for moral values, they were no different from any other show according to James E. Cooper, who had a financial interest in the Barnum organization in 1885 and 1886, "but Barnum always succeeded in making the church and Sunday school people think so."[17] In the full ten years prior to combining with James A. Bailey, under three different sets of management, Barnum's penchant for overstatement and self laudation persisted in the show's advertising. During the 1870s, P. T. Barnum's Greatest Show on Earth was a true reflection of the image P. T. Barnum had invented for himself.

&

James A. Bailey, who was beyond doubt the greatest showman of nineteenth century American circuses, first appeared in a title of one in 1875. From that year until the time of this writing, his presence, along with P. T. Barnum's, has remained in public view on handbills, lithographs, newspaper columns and all other forms of circus advertising.

James Anthony Bailey was short in stature, slender and wiry, a bundle of nerves, and a tireless worker—or as his employees put it, "a worker from workville." He was completely wrapped up in his circus, wrestling with the minutest details of it's management from morning until night. He was one of the most approachable of men. "The humblest 'super' with a grievance [did] not fear to lay it before him, and, if a just one, it [was] remedied."[18] He had a kindly disposition, but was a strict disciplinarian, requiring everyone to do their work according to his expectations. "The rules that he made for his employees—prohibiting drunkenness, smoking about the show, immorality, personal uncleanliness (sic), fighting, or insolence to patrons—none of the employees dare[d] violate, for there [was] a fine for the first offense and absolute dismissal for the second."[19] He was a physical wonder to his associates. "To every one of his 1,000 employees of the circus his existence [was] personal and ever present, for he [was] always trotting around, giving directions in a calm voice that permit[ed] no dispute, the while giving vent to his surplus energy by twirling a lead pencil between the thumb and fore finger of his left hand."[20] He was shy and secretive, and was opposed to being photographed or interviewed by the press, but preferred to remain unnoticed by the public.

His employees loved him. There were innumerable instances when he sent his personal check to a performer who had been injured or to an employee who had become destitute by sickness.[21] If one of them was too ill to work, his pay was never docked. If there was sickness in the family or some other adversity, he would learn about it and issue a check in an envelope always labeled "strictly confidential."

He was said to have treated his animals as he treated his men. He did not sell his old or worn out stock, but gave them to zoological gardens or kept them at winter quarters for the remainder of their lives. "To abuse a horse was as much as a man's job was worth, and Mr. Bailey watched his horses like a hawk. All that were bought he selected himself, even the draught horses."[22]

Peter McNally, a Bailey acquaintance, gave this succinct explanation for the showman's level of greatness: "He was always the hardest worker in the outfit. He would be first on the lot and last away; always on the move and always knowing everything that went on. His watchword was work; and that with his great brain and his energy and attention to detail were the secrets of his success."[23]

Bailey, whose real name was McGinnis, spent his early years under the most humble of circumstances. He was born in Detroit, Michigan, July 4, 1847, of Scotch-Irish descent. Upon the early death of his parents, at the age of ten he was placed under the care of a guardian.

"I was made to work like a dog," he later revealed. "On the slightest provocation I was whipped. My guardian had boys of my age. For their misdeeds I was punished. I was kept working so hard that I was always late at school, so I was continually being whipped by the teacher and kept after school. Then, for being late at home, I was whipped again."

He withstood such treatment until he was nearly thirteen years old. Then one morning he started down the road, pointed away from home, determined never to return.

"I wore a big straw hat, a little brown jacket and trousers that buttoned to it, and was barefoot. My only possession was a jackknife, with one broken blade."[24]

During this newly found freedom he experienced short periods of employment. Right after leaving Detroit he stopped at a farm house to apply for work and, it being harvesting time, he was hired at $3.25 a month and board. He next remained a few months working at a livery stable. Finally he ended up in Pontiac, Michigan, as bellboy at the Hodges House.

On June 17, 1860, he was introduced to the world of the arena when he met Fred Bailey and Benjamin Stevens, agents for the Robinson & Lake circus. The men were stopping at the hotel as they worked in advance of the show. Anxious to make something of himself, young McGinnis asked for a job. Bailey, who had taken a liking to him, hired him as an apprentice advertiser. The name of McGinnis was quickly changed to that of the boy's mentor and benefactor. The juvenile advertiser remained with Robinson & Lake until 1864 when at seventeen, perhaps for the winter lay-off, he became an advertising agent for the Duffield & Flynne theatre in Nashville, which included such ancillary duties as ticket seller and usher.

Here again opportunity intervened. One evening a man by the name of Green, a sutler in the 14th Army Corps, serving the 114th Ohio Regiment, attended the theatre. The place was packed with soldiers, as it usually was during the war years, so Green had to settle for standing room. Once inside he presented young usher Bailey with a tip of five dollars for a seat. Bailey refused the money, explaining that the only place to buy tickets was at the box office. This expression of honesty made an impression on Green, and a few weeks later he offered Bailey a position as his clerk. The lad accepted and remained a sutler's clerk until the end of the war, participating in all of the battles from Chattanooga to Atlanta.

In 1866 Bailey re-entered the circus business. He joined Lake's Hippo-Olympiad as assistant agent and chief bill poster, working under his old friend Benjamin Stevens. Two years later, at the young age of 21, he became the general agent for the show, a position he held through 1869. On August 21 of that summer William Lake was shot and killed at Granby, Missouri, by a local bully who had attempted to sneak into the concert. Bailey remained for the end of the season, at which time the organization was terminated.

Having saved a small amount of money, he leased the concert privileges of Hemmings, Cooper & Whitby for the 1870 tour. This move began a relationship with proprietor James E. Cooper that lasted for the next ten years. Together, but with Bailey's budding genius, they would gradually transform a commonplace circus into the most competitive arenic organization in the world.

I
MR. BARNUM'S DEBUT

"THIS ENTERPRISE WILL COMBINE—AS all
my shows have aimed to do—wholesome instruction with innocent amusement; will in every particular be moral and unexceptionable. Everything
will be new. The exhibition will contain more startling and
entirely novel wonders of creation than were ever before
seen in one collection, as I expect to make this the crowning
success of my managerial life." These words, written by P.
T. Barnum in the show's first Advance Courier would prove
prophetic.

P. T. Barnum's Great Traveling Museum, Menagerie,
Caravan and Hippodrome was a formidable newcomer when
it left New York in April of 1871. The size of the investment is unclear. Coup has stated that the partners "began
with $300,000 worth of stuff."[1] Others have estimated the
initial capitalization as being somewhere between $400,000
and $500,000. Barnum wrote that he was to foot the bills,
but Castello reported that the three men contributed $60,000
each.[2] It may be that Coup and Castello put up that amount,
which could have included equipment from their 1870 circus; but considering the $100,000 Barnum had previously
incurred, it is quite probable that he supplied the majority of
money. This can be supported by a letter that Barnum sent
to the "Flatfoots," his later partners, dated September 2,
1877, in which he stated that "when Coup, Castello and myself first started I owned considerably more than half...."[3]

Whatever the division of investment, Barnum had himself a good deal. He controlled two-thirds of the company. He had a guaranteed bonus of up to $10,000 for the use of his name. He had sole rights to the sale of his autobiography, less the value of the free ticket provided with each. The books, which cost him nine cents apiece and retailed for $1.50, were sold by the tens of thousands. To protect these interests, Barnum appointed his ex-son-in-law, S. H. Hurd, as treasurer.

In total, the size and expense of this new organization was far beyond anything offered in the past. There were three large exhibition tents, separating the menagerie, the museum, and the arena, an innovation this year shared only by J. E. Warner's Great Pacific Circus.[4] There were between five and eight horse tents holding about thirty head of baggage stock each and a dining tent along with a wagon fitted up to be a cookhouse. The total spread of canvas covered nearly three acres. The entire aggregation moved in ninety-five to one hundred wagons pulled by 245 horses, driven by 175 teamsters. To complete the complement, there were sixty arenic performers and seventy-five other employees.

We do not know the size of the main tent; but at the outset it was still a round top, much larger than the other two, and probably larger than what was being used by other circuses. Our guess is that the show started out with about a 125 foot canvas, which seated some 5,000 people. On April 27, during the show's third week on the road, the Newark *Daily Advertiser* announced that the tent had been expanded to accommodate 7,400.[5] This could have been accomplished by replacing the original round top with another somewhat larger, or simply by adding seating to the existing space. Let it be noted that claims of audience sizes varied greatly. Seating capacity figures and audience attendance counts were generally arrived at through conjecture and, unless there is specific boxoffice accounting, should be accepted accordingly.

The cost of operation was unprecedented in the circus business, with daily expenditures amounting to as much as $2,500. Other circus managers scoffed at the sheer madness of the Barnum people. Such an extravagant combination, they jeered, could never be made to turn a profit and would certainly "break to pieces from unwieldy weight" and fall into ruin. Future events would prove these circus sages wrong.

The layout of the 1871 Barnum Advance Courier is indicative of Barnum's interests in his three circus departments. Ten columns of the sixteen page, four-column per page publication was used for describing the museum, eight columns for the menagerie, and but three for the arenic performance (and six and a half for himself).

The museum was the most outstanding feature and marked the first time that a real exhibition of its kind was connected with a circus. It is true that sideshows had presented oddities and exotic acts similar to what one would find in a museum, but the Barnum circus museum was far, far more representative, more expansive, and, one might add, more expensive to operate. It was a typical Barnum accumulation of "humbug," oddities, and educational items.

Several of the major attractions were introduced in the Advance Courier. The live exhibition was headed by San Francisco born Admiral Dot (whose real name was Leopold Kahn). He was described as a midget smaller than Tom Thumb, twenty-five inches in height and weighing a mere fifteen pounds. Purported at this time to be twelve years of age, he was dressed in a British naval uniform as he sang, danced, and played on drums. Alongside him, making him look even more diminutive, was the French giant, Mons. Goliath. The Courier alleged he was the "tallest man in the

Admiral Dot

world," standing eight feet, ten inches in height, every part of which was well proportioned. There was Miss Anna E. Leake, a young lady born without arms, who demonstrated her astounding ability to crochet, embroider, sew, use sissors, fork and knife, drink from a tumbler, and write, all with her toes. It was said that her writing was finer than most people could accomplish with their hands. The Infant Esau, another Barnum phenomenon, was a bearded child, said to be but five years of age. She was described as covered with hair from her head to her feet, including a perfectly developed moustache and side whiskers.

In addition to live curiosities, there was an array of mechanical figures assembled by Wesley L. Jukes. Jukes, a native of Pittsburgh, met Barnum in 1870 when he was a glass blower at Wood's Museum in New York City. A man of unique invention, he was placed in charge of devising the mechanical figures, automatic music, and other contrivances of the Barnum circus museum. During the next five years he received $250 a week for devoting his efforts to developing and overseeing the maintenance of these various automatons.

The most prominent of the lot were the life-size figures of "The Dying Zouave" and "The Sleeping Beauty." The former was draped in a French Zouave military uniform, breathing and struggling from the effects of a fatal bullet, while the wound remitted a stream of blood. "The Sleeping Beauty's" chief attraction was her ability to breath precisely as if alive.

There was also a mechanical supporting cast. "The Magic Drummer" bowed to his curious on-lookers, then answered questions in arithmetic, geography, and history. He was programmed to pick from the audience the "handsomest lady and gentleman," and accomplish remarkable feats on the drum from a selection of tunes.

Competing in making racket was an "Automatic Trumpeter," an invention of a Mons. Maelzel. The instrumentalist moved its hands, arms, head, body, and trumpet, all of which had cost Barnum and enriched the Frenchman to the amount of $10,000.

Alongside the above were a covey of seven lady bell ringers, all automated, all life-like; a flock of beautiful birds, fully plumed and elaborately mechanized to sing, warble, and flutter. A full size goat, deceptively real, nourished her kid, bleated, and ate hay. A rendition of "The Last Supper" contained moving figures visually arranged in imitation of the great masters. "The Mechanical Leotard," constructed by Professor Pepper of the Royal Polytechnic Institute of London expressly for the Barnum organization, was a marvel of gears that powered the figure through a routine of balancing, vaults, and somersaults. Add to this a rabbit that played the tambourine, a monkey violinist, and a musical cat and dog, all products of human engineering.

There was a legion of other exhibits, quiet and immovable. Within the museum tent were wax figures, a Hall of Armor, an Egyptian mummy, a 3,000 year old Eskimo clothed in the seals of his homeland, relics of "cannibals," a rapid fire artillery piece from the Franco-Prussian war that shot 600 rifle balls per minute, an assortment of Oriental curiosities, a jawbone and teeth of a whale, a taxidermist's world of natural history, a slice of trunk with bark thirty-one inches thick from a California tree—"in the interior of which a score of people can stand," and much, much more. One source credits the show with transporting all this in twenty vans, constructed to be opened on the side for displaying the items.

The menagerie, second in importance, was sufficient to support its advertising "puffery." It consisted of twelve camels, four lions, a rhinoceros, zebras, two elephants (one

large, one small), gnus, yaks, elands, tawny and black leopards, kangaroos, white deer, boars, various birds, and monkeys—in all, enough beasts to fill thirty cages. Some time
during the tour sea lions arrived in tanks from Alaska, cost-
ing the show $9,000 up front and even more throughout the
season, since they existed exclusively on fish, requiring 300
pounds a day to satisfy their oceanic appetites.[6]

The ring performance was the least spectacular of the
three exhibitions. The roster included very few names of
lasting importance, with many appearing to be European im-
ports. Mlle. Pauline Hindley (who was killed this first year
by a fall from a horse in Rome, New York), Mrs. Dan Castello, Mlle. Carlotta DaVinci, Maria Celeste Girardeau, and
the Marion Sisters were the equestriennes. In the male tumbling, leaping, gymnastic, acrobatic, and riding departments,
there was a list of "unfamiliars" that included such names as
Smith, English, Cook, Hartnette, Giovani, Fitzgerald, and
Heimberger, perhaps confirming the allegation that English,
French, German, and Italian artists had been secured especially for P. T. Barnum's great hippodrome.

There were, however, some performers well known
to American audiences. They were William Dutton, a much-
traveled and respected pad and bareback rider; the flying
gymnastic team of David R. Hawley and Thomas E. Miaco;
Burnell Runnells and his sons, Bonnie and Freddie, gymnasts and athletes; and Dan Castello, who presented his trick
horse, Czar, and a pair of comic mules, Artemus and Timo-
thy. Surprisingly, no clowns were listed in the Advance
Courier. This could have been a Barnum decision, because
clowns received much of the blame from circus detractors
for vulgarizing the performance.

The street procession was more than adequate. The
Brooklyn *Eagle* described the magnificent spectacle as "a

bewildering variety of cars, chariots, splendid horses, a vehicle drawn by a long train of camels, horsemen in gorgeous
costumes, ponies, banners, paintings, mirrors, carving and
gilding, the whole stretching near a mile in length."[7] It was
led by a bandwagon, the "Car of Oberon" drawn by ten camels—a vehicle about twelve feet long and eight feet wide,
richly decorated in green and gold, the sides inlaid with mirrors.   Upon this enormous imported English car, rode, in
tableau vivant, living figures, male and female, including a
lady occupying the "pinnacle of fame" resting some forty
feet from the ground. Following in order were the ring
horses; Tom Thumb's miniature carriage drawn by Shetland
ponies and driven by juveniles; thirty highly ornamented
cages of varying colors, on top of one a large automated rose
bud that unfolded leaf by leaf revealing a cupid in the center,
and on another an automated horizontal bar performer. Then
came the "Temple of Juno," twenty-eight or thirty feet high,
the top surmounted by a golden canopy, the sides lined with
mirrors ten feet long and five feet wide, richly decorated
with animals, birds, dragons, etc. The two elephants completed the procession.

The opening date, April 10 through 15, was in Brooklyn at the Fulton Avenue lot. Attendance was immense from the outset, which prompted the New York *Clipper* to express amazement that "never did a company start out with such a successful week's work as did Barnum's show in Brooklyn," the total attendance being estimated at not less than 60,000.[8] This marked the beginning of the greatest circus success story to date.

The tour was confined to the northeastern states where the Barnum name was most familiar. From Brooklyn, the routing took the show into New Jersey, Connecticut, Massachusetts, Rhode Island, New Hampshire, Maine, Vermont, and, from August 21 until closing, the state of New York, with the final stand in Harlem on October 28. The itinerary was mostly made up of the larger cities because the show was so expensive to run. Being transported by horse and wagon for the complete tour meant that occasionally it was necessary to make jumps of thirty to forty miles between stands. When this occurred, sometimes the ring stock was shipped by rail.[9] When it was necessary to perform in the

less populated communities in order to break up a long jump, the management had to be satisfied with lesser receipts. Coup has written that the daily income ranged from $1,000 to $7,000.

Throughout the season the show played to record-breaking business. In most of the places three performances were given daily—10 a.m., 2 p.m. and 8 p.m. at the longer stands; 10 a.m., 1 p.m., and 7 p.m. at the one-day stops. There were many times when even these were not enough. At the Newark, New Jersey, evening performance of April 28, every seat and every available space for standing room was occupied well before 8 o'clock, totaling a full 5,000 bodies; the ticket office was closed and the crowd outside the tent refused admission.[10] The three performances in Portland, Maine, were attended by 15,000 people. In Rochester, New York, there were 9,000 at a single show. Compare this success to others that year: at a Hartford stand L. B. Lent's circus grossed $2,470 on the day, and Stone & Murray, $1,760; but Barnum's was an impressive $8,650.[11]

Success in Maine alone surprised everyone. The village of Waterville overflowed on July 29 with people who had come from as far as seventy-five miles in carriages, wagons, ox carts, and on foot. Some brought their own tents and camped overnight. The sale of intoxicating beverages was banned for the day, but barrels of water and supplies of ice were placed on street corners free to the public. To resolve this unexpected phenomenon Coup and company decided on a continuous exhibition, with one act following another in the ring without stop until 9 p.m. At that hour a heavy rainfall furnished an excuse for cessation. Fortunately the following day was Sunday, an open date. Still, an exhausted troupe of men, women, and horses had to travel the forty-eight miles to Lewiston, where on Monday three shows were scheduled.[12] This was the first time a circus had ever given continuous performances in this way. Encouraged by such a reception, the management intended to go as far east as Bangor; but such planning was soon changed because too few of the smaller towns were deemed large enough to break up the lengthy jump. The fact that several bridges en route were not sufficient to accommodate the larger chariots was an even more convincing deterrent.

Another example of success was the two-day Albany stand. The show was in conflict with Dan Rice's Paris Pavilion Circus, which was there from August 21 through the 24th. Rice's outfit was the high-class wooden and canvas structure that was originally built for the Paris Exposition of 1867. It was furnished with parquet seating, private boxes, and a family circle, comfortable cane-bottomed chairs, and elaborate gas lighting. This was certainly a novelty that invited a good deal of attention. The pavilion was set up on a midtown lot. Barnum's tent was at the outskirts of town. On the other hand, Rice had only an arenic performance—no menagerie, museum, or sideshow, and no street procession.

His pavilion, accommodating well over 3,000 spectators, was scaled at $1.00, 75¢, and 50¢. The Barnum people were getting 50¢ for the full package. And to add impetus to the rivalry, Barnum came over from Bridgeport for the engagement to address the audiences personally.

Surprisingly, both circuses did well. The Barnum show was in Albany on the 22nd and 23rd, in the middle of Rice's stand. A hard rain came down on the 21st leaving the lot a mire of mud, and threatening weather carried over into the next day. Yet, referring to the performance at the Paris Pavilion on the 22nd, an Albany *Argus* correspondent wrote, "The vast amphitheatre was filled from parquet to the most extreme standing aisles of the family circle."

And of the Barnum show, on the opening day "nearly eight thousand people, from every walk in life, attended the afternoon performance, and in the evening the rush was almost overwhelming."[13] On the 23rd, people from Coxsackie and adjoining towns chartered a steamer, and others came by wagons and railroad to see the great show.

For this stand W. C. Coup used nearly 20,000 feet of lumber for extra seating.[13] This is the first mention of local lumber purchases for temporary bleachers. It will not be the last.

At Utica, attendance for the August 31 stand was estimated by the *Daily Observer* to be from 12,000 to 18,000 for the three performances. "Suppose that even the lowest of these estimates was exaggerated," the article read, "say that only 10,000 paying patrons visited the show; then Mr. Barnum received five thousand dollars from the sale of tickets.... We make no account of his profits from side shows, sales of fruits, lemonade, photographs, &c." The piece ended with: "Barnum's show is a good thing for Barnum."[14]

A particular concern of the contracting agent was the selection of sites for the tents to be erected. Some of the

larger cities had grounds on which shows traditionally performed. But as urban centers grew in size and population,
open spaces in downtown areas became almost extinct; creating a necessity for circuses to rely on local transit facilities.
By the 1860s most U.S. cities had franchised horse or mule-
powered street railways.[15] Care had to be taken to find show
lots within a comfortable distance from these transportation
systems.

A device that greatly contributed to the show's success was the use made of railroad excursion trains. Reduced
fares which included the price of a ticket allowed people in
the out-lying areas to easily travel to the circus grounds and,
once there with ticket in hand, avoid waiting in line. The
idea of excursion trains was not original with the Barnum
circus; an advertisement announcing them in connection with
the Rivers & Derious show appeared as early as 1855.[16]
What Coup did, however, was to make excursions a continuing policy, contracting with the rail companies wherever
tracks were available. The result was that the crowds inside
the tent were often greater than the entire population of the
municipalities in which the show was exhibiting. At the previously mentioned Waterville stand, for example, a train of
twenty-seven cars brought patrons from Bangor, some fifty
miles distant. On the same day a string of fourteen cars arrived by rail from Skowhegan and seventeen from Belfast.
Receipts from the three exhibitions that day totaled over
$7,000.[17]

The New York *Clipper* called these the greatest successes ever achieved in the sawdust circle:

There are few men that have the courage to invest nearly a half a million of dollars in so precarious a business, and to run it at a daily expense of nearly twenty-five hundred dollars. But Mr. Barnum had
faith that the public would respond liberally to his appeal. One great

Ben Lusbie

secret of his success has been ever to give the public a great deal for their money, and to fix the prices of admission at popular rates.[18]

An interesting footnote to the season was the emergence of Ben Lusbie as an unusual attraction. He began his career as a telegrapher for the Erie Railroad, but re-occupied himself to ticket seller for Burton's Theatre in New York City. In 1861 he was employed for the same line of work at Barnum's museum, where he established a reputation as a "Lightning Ticket Seller." When Barnum entered the circus business this year, Lusbie became the man in the boxoffice.

Going on the road increased his fame. The great P. T. Barnum show of 1871, with a seating capacity of twice that of any other circus, and with the enormous crowds that flocked to three performances daily, created the challenge and the proper platform for public acknowledgment. And the exuberant press agentry that contributed substantially to the show's success elevated Lusbie into a star and ultimately a place on the bills alongside names of the featured performers. The Boston *Herald* said of him: "There are some things which people will not believe without ocular demonstration; therefore we cannot reasonably expect our readers to credit our statement that this vendor of pasteboards will take the money, make the necessary change for and deliver a hundred tickets a minute into the uplifted hands of the multitude beneath his window, do it for an hour together and never make a mistake." Amazement was expressed in the Boston *Times* as well: "Barnum's lightning ticket seller ranks as one of the 'living curiosities'.... It is said that he has often sold eight thousand tickets in an hour, but what is more remarkable is the fact that, when through, the receipts invariably correspond with the tickets sold. Where the money goes and where the change comes from is a mystery, but the rapidity of his movements suggests the suspicion that steam and intricate mechanism are in some manner applied to his physical make-up."[19]

After a short lay-off from touring, the show moved into the Empire Rink, 63rd Street and Third Avenue, New York City, for a winter engagement that lasted from November 13 to January 6. The ring was the centerpiece of the large enclosure, with the museum items aligned on the right side as one entered and the menagerie on the left. The performing animals were in the rear. For opening night at least, Admiral Dot, the French Giant and other oddities, as well as Barnum himself, circulated among the audience, creating a welcoming atmosphere. The doors were open from morning to night, which allowed patrons to attend the menagerie and museum exhibits at any hour. This would be the first of five consecutive post-season appearances conducted by the Barnum people in that city. In so doing, winter storage was either shortened or eliminated, the circus personnel were given employment for most of the year, and, if business proved favorable, there would be ample start-up money come spring.

This initial year of a Barnum designated circus destroyed traditional notions. It gave proof that a large show, properly managed, could make a profit. It revealed the value of an expansive museum which, along with an adequate menagerie, served as an alternative to the circus for those who were adverse to attending an arenic performance. It demonstrated the feasibility of advertising within a much wider perimeter to bring in an audience from greater distances than had been previously attempted. And it established the use of inter-urban railway systems to make this possible. The "proof of the pudding was in the eating"; and, according to Coup, at season's end the show had made "a half-million even."[20]

This was a milestone within the historical progression of the American circus. It served as the impetus for real growth, both by example and through the stimulus of competition, a growth that would continue for the rest of the century. Without Barnum's money, his name, his vision, and his need to remain within the limelight of public adulation, this might not have occurred, which alone justifies the conjoining of that name with "circus" for all time.

&

Election years usually provide a distraction for the entertainment business. Although the year of 1872 was first-rate for President Grant, who was re-elected by a 760,000 majority, the largest ever polled by a presidential candidate, it was not good for circuses. To make matters worse, there was a late spring which caused the wagon shows to get a delayed start because of bad roads. Hot summer weather, especially in the West, kept the crowds down until the whole country experienced a severe cold spell in October. Ten of forty-five circuses closed early. There were rumors that some shows had planned to reduce their admission charges to twenty-five cents, but I found no evidence that this occurred.

The Barnum show, despite the conditions stated above, grossed a million dollars with profits exceeding $200,000, the first circus to ever achieve such an amount.[21] There were three ticket wagons on the Barnum lot this year, one of which was reserved for ladies (women's suffrage being a hot issue). And they were kept busy. Twenty-eight thousand admissions were sold in Cleveland in two days. In Sandusky, Ohio (population 13,000), there were 26,000 sales for three performances. In Harrisburg, Pennsylvania, attendance reached 30,000. So much money was being shipped east by the circus—shipped under W. C. Coup's name—that the express company suspected it was the profits of a gambling operation and had their detectives investigate. All this gave support to the designation of "Greatest Show on Earth," used for the first time this season.

This year, 1872, was also the season when the Barnum circus first went on rails, an inspiration of which both Barnum and Coup have claimed the authorship. "Perceiving that my great combination was assuming such proportions that it would be impossible to move it by horse power," Barnum wrote, "I negotiated with all the railway companies between New York and Omaha, Nebraska, for the transportation by rail of my whole show."[22] A Coup statement contradicted this when he disclosed that he was mentally fatigued by "his partner's opposition and his requests to abandon the scheme."[23] Nevertheless, it was Coup who worked out the complex arrangements and made it happen. But what about Dan Castello? He was the only one of the partners who had had prior experience with using rail travel. Unfortunately, there is no record to explain what input Castello shared in this development.

The change-over to rail was considered necessary in order to avoid playing the small towns in which attendance was limited. By using the railroad, "we could ignore the small places," Coup explained, "and travel only from one big town to another, thereby drawing the cream of the trade from the adjacent small towns instead of trying to give an exhibition in each."[24] And, advantageously, longer jumps could be made between dates and still allow time for three performances a day.

At first the show leased cars from the railroad companies on whose tracks they traveled, but as the season progressed they were replaced by circus-owned cars built to a standard size to facilitate loading. There were sixty-five of them at the start, divided into two trains. Just how they were loaded and unloaded during this trial year has never been fully explained; although Coup has commented on the laborious process of teaching the workmen a proficient method. "It is a positive fact that I never took the clothes from my back from the time of first loading until we reached Philadelphia, our seventh stop."[25]

Fred Dahlinger, Jr., has, however, unearthed a newspaper account that describes the 1873 Barnum show system and which may have been similar to 1872. It stated that the first wagon was "drawn through the entire train of open cars and the others follow[ed] afterwards." It was made possible by the use of metal plates that served as runways from one car to the next. For unloading there were ramps from which the forward cars could descend by means of rope and pulleys controlled by horse power. This end-loading method, where wagons were pulled one by one down the string of flats, became a standard in the industry.[26]

The commitment to rail travel necessitated the creation of a new position, that of "railroad contractor." In his memoirs Coup wrote that routes were generally completed no later than the first of February of each year, at which time the railroad contractor went to work. We can assume much or all of this first year on rails for the Barnum show was arranged by Coup himself in pre-season. He claims to have telegraphed the superintendents of the various railroads, asking for accommodations and guarantees of on-time arrivals. "After a great deal of correspondence," he wrote in his notes, "I went to Philadelphia and interviewed the officials of the Pennsylvania Company. I urged and argued and argued and urged ... and I hung on until I finally made arrangements with them."[27]

The designation of "railroad contractor" does not appear in company rosters immediately. The Barnum route book for 1872 does, however, list Charles C. Pell as "railroad

manager"; but the route book for the following year makes
no specific mention of any agent in charge of railroads. The
precise use of the term does not appear until 1874 when
George R. Bronson is listed as "railroad contractor" for the
Great Eastern and Frank Keigh for the L. B. Lent circus.[28]

We are given an insight to the often frustrating job of
contracting with rail companies from at letter dated November 17, 1878, to John Parks, manager of Howes' Great London. The letter was written by Lewis B. Lent, then contractor for that circus. Lent was a man of many years in the
business, most of that time as proprietor of his own show.
He was well versed in the ins and outs of touring.

In the letter he wrote bitterly about his dealings with
the Superintendent of the Charlotte, Columbia & Augusta
Railroad, a Mr. Kline. He complained about the high rates
being levied and his unsuccessful attempt to convince Kline
that the show could not pay those amounts. He accused the
railroad company of not transporting anything that paid them
50 per cent of the rate they were charging the circus.
"[Kline] put in the cotton plea that they had more cotton than
they could haul, were short of engines, and if they took the
Great London they would have to haul off two cotton trains
that were paying them big money." Lent then responded
with "if they wanted to drive the show patronage from their
road they had succeeded" and that he "could not and would
not pay any such ruinous rates," thereupon he left the office.

Contracting for the Barnum show was no less frustrating. The daily average rates for moving the train of sixty
cars (six of them passenger coaches) ranged from $600 to
$1,000.[29]

The whole of the second season of operation was
much the same as in 1871. There was no necessity to add to
or change the museum and menagerie because the show was
traveling a different route. The policy of three shows a day

Fiji Cannibals.

was continued. Barnum's autobiography was still being sold for $1.50, which included a ticket to the circus. Barnum, of course, held the title of proprietor and general director, and W. C. Coup as manager. The Advance Courier listed Dan Castello as manager of the Grand Oriental Circus and S. Q. Stokes as the superintendent of the hippodrome. Treasurer Ben Lusbie still amazed ticket buyers with his dexterity, as the man from the Evansville *Journal* exclaimed: "To see him take money with one hand and reach for change and tickets with another is almost as much a sight as to see the armless woman write with her toes."[30]

New to the museum, however, displayed in the tent with the other living curiosities, were the "Fiji Cannibals," representing the first non-American exhibit of ethnicity within the circus. There were four in number, all genuine Fijans. Two of the men were of normal stature, the third was a dwarf, who died after only a few weeks in show business. The fourth, a woman, was well educated and served as a translator. Barnum claimed in his autobiography that the group had been "ransomed at great cost from the hands of a royal enemy, into whose hands they had fallen, and by whom they were about to be killed and perhaps eaten,"[31] which, of course, was utter nonsense.

The Fijans were quite an attraction. The South Pacific was exotic and mysterious to most Americans, and the Fiji islands, located approximately 3,100 miles southwest of Hawaii, was particularly intriguing. Their society was highly stratified and warfare was common as leaders competed for control. Cannibalism sometimes occurred between rival tribes; which, in the Western world became the accepted stereotype for the entire population. Consequently, the billing exacerbated the notion with such verbiage as "Wild Fiji Cannibals, Captives of war, lately ransomed from King Thokam, by Mr. Barnum, at a cost of $15,000." The men were displayed, as one might expect, in full native attire, bare to the waist, war-like in appearance, to engender the appropriate amount of ferocity. The woman was spared such indignity. Reportedly, she "looked very much like any other molasses colored woman with her wool spread out."[32]

Add to this a display of American aborigines, the so-called "Digger Indians," desert dwellers from the Great Basin. The disparaging sobriquet is derived from their mode of survival—the gathering of seeds and grasshoppers, digging roots, capturing lizards from their holes, etc. The inclusion of this exhibit may have been influenced by Barnum's friend, Samuel Clemens, in his book *Roughing It*, written a decade earlier. "It was along this wild country, and far from any habitation of white men ..." he wrote in reference to this breed, "that we came across the wretchedest type of mankind I have ever seen, up to this writing." Indeed, public curiosity was stirred by their most primitive and destitute life style, imposed by the barren and demanding nature of their environment. However, a description in the Advance Courier leads one to question their authenticity. It promised "practical illustrations of the method of lassooing wild buffalo, hunting, modes of warfare and many other curious entertainments of savage life," examples far akin to the normal activity of the "Diggers."

The street procession, too, was much the same as in 1871. Two agents familiar with the parade route led the cortege in a buggy, followed by an elegant wagon devoted to the sale of Barnum's autobiography. Then came the "Orpheus Bandwagon" pulled by twelve camels and four horses. Next, the twenty cages, each with a four-horse hitch. Some of these had automata on top, as they had the year before. There were several ponies ridden by boys after which appeared Admiral Dot's miniature coach pulled by four ponies. The large, revolving "Temple of Juno" with a ten-camel hitch followed; then some twenty mounted men wearing suits of armor; there was another band, apparently hired locally at each stand; and finally more cages and the two elephants. Somewhere in the line was a glass-enclosed snake den, the first such cage to appear on American streets. The anacondas and boa constrictors within were performed during the procession by snake charmer Zaldid Abdeldare.

The menagerie was not the largest on the road, but it contained some of the rarest animals. There was the only giraffe in the country at this time and perhaps the largest African lion ever witnessed in America. An East Indian tapir

was a new addition; according to advertising, the first to be
brought to this country. The beast was quite an attraction,
probably well worth the alleged cost of $11,000.

The quality of the ring performances was much improved from the previous year. James Melville, one of the
leading bareback riders of his day, was there with his sons,
Clarence, George, Frank, and Donald. For the principal act,
there was the twelve year old Katie Stokes, the most physi-
cally beautiful equestrienne of her day. And let us not ignore
"Barnum's new Educated Riding Goat," Alexis—purportedly trained in Egypt and imported at a cost of $10,000 (reveal-
ing how far Barnum would go to get someone's goat)—that
demonstrated its ability to stay atop a horse.[33]

The show had ten tents on the lot, four of them presumably for horses and equipment. There were four that
housed the exhibitions and that could be entered for a single

Above: Morris H. Porter photograph of the P. T. Barnum layout taken while the show was in Kalamazoo, Michigan, on October 24, 1872.
Below: Enlargement of the big top from the above picture, showing two center poles.

Stereoview of the 1872 P. T. Barnum circus tent interior, entered into the Library of Congress in 1873 by the photographer, A. W. Anderson. This picture confirms the use of two center-poles and shows a single ring with space enough around it to accommodate the grand entrée.

50¢ admission. One tent displayed the automatons and wax figures, as well as the living curiosities; caged animals were in another; led animals in still another; and the last was occupied by the ring. In a normal set-up, a lot space of 393 by 208 feet was required.[34] A Morris H. Porter photograph taken while the show was in Kalamazoo, Michigan, on October 24, shows the big top with two center poles.[35] There is also a stereoview representing the interior of the 1872 tent, entered into the Library of Congress in 1873 by the photographer, A. W. Anderson. It confirms the use of two center-poles and shows a single ring with space enough around it to accommodate the grand entrée. Using the picture, noted circus engineer, R. S. MacDougall, estimated the canvas to be a 190 (plus or minus) foot round top with a 60-70 foot middle piece.[36]

Although the advertising boasted of the admission to these six tents for one ticket price, the Annex, which occupied the sixth tent, required the payment of an additional 15¢. The inclusion of this auxiliary entertainment was designed, in part, to drive away the irresponsible sideshow attractions that have in the past followed circuses as "sharks follow a ship." The proprietors of this establishment were the Bunnell brothers, John W. and George B., natives of Southport, Connecticut. They entered show business at an early age and gained experience in its various forms. At this point they controlled New York's New American Museum at Broadway and 9th Street, from where they acquired most of the exhibits for the Annex. George had been a museum manager for Barnum for several years. Agent John Dingess said of him, "To judge from his appearance and conversation, one would deem him an ordinary tradesman who feared that the wolf was hard by his door, and from the spectators at his museum and his bank account he would be set down at a quarter of a million."[37]

This engraving from the P. T. Barnum 1872 Advance
Courier depicts the grand entrée spectacle called The
Halt in the Desert. It was purported to include a caravan
of 24 Bactrian camels and dromedaries, a herd of baby
elephants, 40 Arabian horses and ponies, Turks, Arabs,
Moors, Mamelukes, Cannibals, knights in armor, and
ladies of the harem, forming an Oriental tourmament in
which over 100 men, women, and children appeared "IN
THE RING AT ONE TIME." This agrees with the conclusion that there was only a single ring in 1872. Just
imagine the grand entrées at this time all crowded into
such limited space.

It has previously been suggested that the 1872 Barnum show originated the use of a second ring for circus performances. As we can see from the illustrations, this is absolutely incorrect. In part, the confusion was caused by advertising that frequently included the line: "The first and only show in the world that uses a double circus ring, and requires a double circus troupe of performers." Such a reference can be found in newspapers from Clinton, Iowa, to Baltimore, Maryland. In the Toledo *Blade* it was stated that "there are seen at one time in the great double ring, in the Grand Entrée Pageant, one hundred performers," etc.[38] The *Journal* of Lodi, Wisconsin, also included reference to "a double set of performers, a double circus ring." Notice that the term "double ring" is used, rather than "two rings." The former could be interpreted to mean one inside the other, the latter to mean rings side by side. The fact is that with the canvas enlarged and elongated, there was space around the single ring. It is safe to assume that the second 1872 ring was not one of two rings, side by side, where simultaneous performances were given; but rather, it was an outer ring in which, for the first time in an American circus, the grand entrée expanded from the confinement of the performing ring to a new-born hippodrome track.

The huge amount of territory covered throughout the season emphasized the advantage of effective rail travel. The tour opened at the Empire Rink in New York City for two weeks. The show then took a lengthy trek through the states of New Jersey, Delaware, Maryland, Pennsylvania, West Virginia, Ohio, Kentucky, Indiana, Illinois, Missouri, Kansas, Iowa, Minnesota, Wisconsin, and Michigan.

The excitement encountered at each stand was even greater than in 1871. "It is safe to say that no similar exhibition ever attracted such elegant audiences as have been

drawn to Belair lot during the week to witness the performance of Mr. Barnum's grand consolidation," wrote a review-
er for the Baltimore *American and Commercial Advertiser*.[39]
The Cleveland papers echoed this sentiment, announcing an
attendance of 28,000 in a single day, with thousands turned
away. "Nothing like such a rush to a tent show has ever been
known in this section of the country at least."[40] Opening
night in Cincinnati on July 16 drew a crowd of 10,640, with
many attendees unable to pass through the gates.[41] The October Chicago stand was similarly reported by the *Inter-
Ocean*:

> The success which has attended Barnum's show in this city since the
> first entertainment has been of a most stupendous character and has
> not been equaled in any place in the West where his tents have been
> hitherto pitched. The rush at every performance has greatly over-
> taxed the seating expected of the hippodrome, and large numbers
> have been turned away. In all the history of similar exhibitions, there
> has been no parallel to the throng and popularity which the "great
> moral show" has experienced in Chicago.[42]

Barnum made his periodic visits to the show, confin-
ing them to the largest cities. In a letter to the Rev. George
H. Emerson of April 14, he stated he would be on hand in
Philadelphia, Baltimore, Washington, and Cleveland. As a
man who loved children, he must have particularly enjoyed
his visit to Baltimore. By his own invitation, residents of
various orphan asylums attended a morning show during the
run, at which time he gave a short lecture. He enjoined the
youngsters to observe three cardinal virtues—temperance,
industry, and integrity.

In Cincinnati he appeared in the ring for the matinee
to healthy cheers from the house and made his usual remarks, closing with "If I have succeeded in pleasing you
with my show it will be highly gratifying to me." This was
followed by more demonstrations from the bleachers. He

made his return for the evening performance and was "called out" again, which met with a similar response.[43] The "calling out," we must admit, was often accomplished by members of the company planted in various parts of the arena.

The season closed with a two-day stand in Detroit on October 29 and 30, the tents covering the full area on Grand River Avenue from Third to Fourth Streets. The success here was representative of the entire tour. On opening day morning trains on all the railroads leading to the city brought thousands of people from the interior towns. In the evening, after 12,000 tickets were sold, the doors were closed, leaving some 3,000 disappointed turn-aways.

The occasion was highlighted when early in the performance Dan Castello entered the ring and presented a gold-headed cane to Dr. Asa Berry, the show's veterinarian, a gift from the groomsmen attached to the show. With the honoree at his side, Castello acclaimed before the entire assembly:

> The season of 1872 closes with tomorrow's exhibition in this city, and your employes (sic), numbering some fifty groomsmen, deem this a proper occasion for presenting you with some slight token of their esteem. They know of no more fitting means of doing this than by asking your acceptance of this cane, which they have instructed me to present in their behalf. By this free offering they wish to acknowledge the uniform courtesy of their employer, the kindness and care they have received from you under all the trying circumstances of this arduous campaign just closing. There may be more striking instances of *caning* on record, but none, I trust, that has resulted in less harm, or that can more securely bind the friendship so long existing between you.[44]

A smaller show was formed in Detroit at this time and sent South under the management of P. A. Older, leased to use Barnum's name and partially financed by him. Older had been in the circus business since 1849, when he traded his Janesville, Wisconsin, saw mill for a third interest in the E. F. and J. Mabie show. Since then he had been connected

with Miles Orton and Yankee Robinson and in 1870 and
1871 was sole proprietor of Older's Museum, Circus and
Menagerie.

There was a suggestion that Coup was opposed to the
splitting up of the animals and equipment, but Barnum was
interested in promoting his name in the South. He could not
do it with his own large show because, with his rail car
wheels built for the northern "standard gauge" tracks (4 feet
8½ inches in width), it would be too expensive, time con-
suming and cumbersome for them to be changed to accommodate the "southern gauge" (5 feet in width), still in use
throughout much of the South.[45] The deal appeared to be a
good one for both parties; the Barnum name was expected to
draw large crowds and the surplus animals loaned to Older
would be cared for throughout the winter months.

Meanwhile, the remainder of the animals and ring
stock were shipped from Detroit to New York City where the
Barnum circus opened for the winter at the Hippotheatron on
14th Street. This building had been used for L. B. Lent's
New York Circus since September of 1866 until the Barnum
organization purchased it in the summer of this year. The
place underwent alterations before "the greatest show on
earth" took possession. Soil was excavated to allow the ring
and surrounding seats to be lowered some twelve feet; and a
gallery was added, thereby nearly doubling the seating capacity to about 2,500. The original benches were removed
and replaced by comfortable chairs. A new facade at the entrance, covered with oil paintings characteristic of the entertainment within, partially concealed the iron building from
frontal view.

The circus was advertised to begin on November 11
but the opening was postponed to November 18, due to the
sickness of many of the valuable ring horses. The company

moved into its winter home with much of the summer roster, the headliner still being the Melville family.

Notably, making their American debut on December 16, were Richard H. Dockrill, wife, Elise, and her brother, Joseph Kennebel. Mons. Dockrill performed a *manège* act and was a skilled scenic rider; but he is most remembered for his ability as an equestrian director. Mme. Dockrill received much praise as an attractive and daring equestrienne. While standing bareback on a horse coursing around the ring at full speed, she leaped over banners and jumped through paper covered hoops, an act that was common to many lady riders. Of greater note was her performances on more than one mount. She is said to have been the first woman to ride and drive four horses together. At this engagement she was billed as "The Empress of the Arena," with the advertising offering $10,000 to anyone who could equal her six-horse act. The Dockrills will acquire more importance as our narrative unfolds.

Joseph Kennebel was a French trick clown who performed without words, communicating with his audience through well arranged facial grimaces, oblique nods, finger motions and grotesque attitudes, something new to the American circus. His appearance in the ring was characterized by an item in the New York *Sun*: "He dresses in green with a long point of black hair at each side of his head, and a similar red point in the middle. His face is white and the eyes are shaded with red and a faint black." The writer found pleasure in his "eccentric movements and changes of countenance." He cited the "butterfly act" as an example, wherein a large white butterfly was attached to the end of a whip, and while Kennebel tried to catch it with one hand, he jerked it away with the other." Another amusing antic was accomplished by using a "basket horse," a woven replica of a

steed, as he mimicked the maneuvers of Mons. Dockrill's
trick horse Ellington.

At the Hippotheatron, the animals and curiosities
were stationed around the outer walls of the building and under the seating risers. The newspaper ads listed four giraffes—the "only living giraffes in North America"—lions,
tigers, leopards, camels, sea lions, gorillas, two elephants,
elands, South American tapirs, yaks, ostriches, and polar
bears.

The winter season began successfully, but within six
short weeks tragedy struck. Around 4:00 a.m. on the morning of Tuesday, December 24, as patrolman Raymond of the
15th Precinct was making his rounds, his attention was suddenly startled by cries of "fire!" After running down 14th
Street toward Third Avenue, he discovered smoke billowing
from the building housing Barnum's circus. An alarm
brought several other officers to the scene, who forced open
the doors of the structure to find the whole of the rear portion
of the premises on fire. Shortly, several hook and ladder
companies arrived; but by then the angry flames had spread
with great rapidity throughout the interior and onto the
wooden roof beams. Alas! the walls of the building, constructed of sheets of corrugated iron, became so hot as to
make it impossible for firemen to enter.

Efforts to rescue the valuable animals were only
slightly successful. Two elephants, known as Jennie and
Sam, and a camel were brought out without difficulty. They
were all that could be saved. The cages of animals had been
installed in the building without wheels, which made it impossible for any to be removed. Fortunately, the horses were
stabled in separate quarters on 11th Street; but unfortunately,
the Hippotheatron and adjoining buildings were destroyed
beyond repair. The loss to the Barnum organization was
heavy, a sad ending to an otherwise banner season.

&

The financial problems for circuses were repeated in 1873. Rampant railroad speculation, notably in the field of construction, combined with over expansion in industry, agriculture, and commerce, weakened the country's financial structure, already shaken by the dwindling European demand for farm products. These conditions produced the Panic of 1873. The failure of the banking firm of Jay Cooke on September 18 precipitated a fall in security prices, ultimately affecting national income and leading to substantial unemployment. For traveling shows an additional element of ill fortune was the yellow fever epidemic in the South which created the crowding of a larger number of them within the Middle-West.

The reader will recall that P. A. Older acquired some of the Barnum show and the right to use the Barnum name in the title. His tour opened in Louisville, Kentucky, on November 4, 1872, and then followed a route through Kentucky, Tennessee, Georgia and Louisiana, ending up with financial trouble in New Orleans.[46] An eight-day stand there closed the operation, which was said to have lost Older his life's savings of $60,000. The magical name of "P. T. Barnum" had not appealed to Southern audiences.

Old John Robinson "owned the South." Circuses under his name had covered the territory for years. In opposition to Older, his press department flooded the route in advance with bills and couriers using Barnum's literature, but attaching it to the Robinson show title. When the Barnum advertising was posted, the Southerners rejected it with "that Yankee clock peddler has copied Uncle John's bills word for word."

The Hippotheatron fire occurred while Barnum was in New Orleans to reclaim the circus he had leased to Older.

In his autobiography he makes no disclosure of the Older show's failure; but simply states that he was in New Orleans visiting his Southern show. Conover wrote that Coup was also there at the time. This was confirmed by an item in the New York *Clipper*—both Barnum and Coup went to New Orleans "to look after the interests of Barnum's Southern Museum, Circus and Menagerie." C. G. Sturtevant, quite the contrary, alleged that Coup refused to go.[47] We believe Conover's entry to be correct.

On January 23, Older and J. M. Chandler contracted to buy the show property from Barnum & Co. that had been stored at Algiers, Louisiana, following the termination of Older's lease in December. Because of the planned enlargement of the Barnum show, this was probably redundant equipment. So here P. T. made another of his close deals. The purchase price was $50,000 plus a "rent" of 7% per annum. An advance of $5,000 was given the proprietors to get the show on the road. Older could draw up to $6,000 in salary, Chandler up to $2,000, and they were allowed to keep $2,000 on hand for emergencies. All profits were to be returned daily to the Barnum company in New York. Older and Chandler were required to guarantee funds necessary to provide winter storage, replacing of animals, and re-fitting of the show in the event the debt was not paid in full by the end of the season. Barnum & Co. retained the privilege of placing a man on the show if so desired at the expense of Older & Chandler. The name of P. T. Barnum was not to be used in any way (Louis E. Cooke claimed that it was). Barnum & Co. retained the right of repossessing the rhinoceros for $7,000 if the one they had in New York died before the start of the season. The contract was signed by S. H. Hurd, treasurer, P. T. Barnum & Co., and by P. A. Older and J. M. Chandler.[48]

The deal gave Older re-birth in circus management under the title of Older & Chandler's Trans-Atlantic Circus and Menagerie. But alas! after a tour in Texas, the unfortunate manager folded in Shreveport, Louisiana, hit by the yellow fever epidemic. All of the performers and musicians and several of the attaches managed to board a steamer bound for St. Louis, the last one to leave the city before the quarantine.[49] Older was ruined again. Epitaphs appeared in the New York *Clipper* trade cards, advertising the sale of the Older & Chandler property by John Caldwell of Shreveport and the animals by James Cumpston (including a black Sumatran rhino for $5,000). This was Older's last experience in show business.

Barnum's partners were deeply effected by the burning of the Hippotheatron. According to Arthur Saxon, Coup was ready to forego traveling and treasurer Hurd was distressed by the loss of the $50,000 revenue that the winter show was expected to contribute.[50] The financial damage from the conflagration was $300,000, by Barnum's statement, and there was only $90,000 insurance. But the circus had grossed a million dollars in 1872, which left a profit of about $250,000; and this, combined with the insurance proceeds, was available to rebuild the third of the property that had been lost. Having framed the largest circus in the country in 1871, and having mounted it on the railroads in 1872, the Barnum/Coup forces could only enlarge it in 1873 to surpass what they had already accomplished.

Coup was in charge of rebuilding the 1873 "Greatest Show on Earth," as they now called it. Most of the work was done in New York City. The repairing and redecorating of the 150 wagons (including parade vehicles and cages) was assigned to Fielding & Sons of 41st Street, and Sebastian and Saal on Third Avenue. Higgins, the well-known tent maker, at 192 West Street, made the tents, of which there were twelve, including a big top that would seat 13,000 people. R. S. Walker of Allen Street was given a contact for $15,000 worth of banners and costumes. At the shops of William Cummins & Son in Bergen, New Jersey, flat cars were built or refurbished. Six sleeping cars were converted from passenger coaches at New Haven. In Cleveland enough stock cars for 300 horses were newly built or repaired at the McNary & Claflen works. William Wallace, a taxidermist at 616 Broadway, prepared over 500 birds that were displayed in about twenty museum cages. Poles were made at local shipyards.[51]

To assemble a decent menagerie at this time required a sizable outlay of cash. Single lions in good condition brought about $1,200 to $2,500, depending on size and training. Exceptionally fine specimens had been sold for as much as $7,500. There was a standing offer of $15,000 for a healthy hippopotamus. Elephants were always marketable at prices ranging from $8,000 to $12,000, according to education; and a large one with the notoriety of killing several keepers could bring even more. A rhinoceros drew a price of from $8,000 to $10,000, and more for a double-horned Sumatran. Real Bengal tigers were worth $7,000 a pair; but leopards brought only half as much; and camels, always plentiful, were down among the hundreds in value. The best feathered ostriches went for $500 or less. With the promulgation of the Darwinian theory, there was a rise in the price of monkeys, the African varieties considered to be the most valuable.

The business of maintaining a large menagerie was even more costly. For example, animals consumed from 300 to 500 pounds of meat daily. The average elephant ate 500 pounds of hay, and camels twice the equivalent of horses. Each sea lion did away with 100 pounds of saltwater fish.

Then there was always a loss of specimens through death, both in transport and within their daily habitation.

The 1873 roster of the Barnum administrative and associate personnel officers was much the same as in 1872. William C. Coup was general manager, Dan Castello was in charge of the circus performance, and S. H. Hurd was the treasurer. These three, now each with a twenty percent interest, and Barnum, with forty, made up the show's ownership.[52] The Bunnell Brothers still operated the sideshow. J. L. Hutchinson, a press agent in 1872, was in charge of the sale of Barnum's autobiography, an opportunity which made him a fortune.

Press agent D. S. Thomas, new to the Barnum organization this year, brought with him the idea of conducting newspaper people on a tour behind the scenes before the matinee of opening day. The benefits of such a feature took the form of full columns of free press reports written by appreciative scribes, and far more interesting to the local readership than display advertising. Agent Thomas continued to do this throughout his several years with the organization.

> Mr. Thomas displayed no zoological pedantry, nor was he oppressive in his official attentions; and yet the newspapermen were induced to see everything and see it for what it was worth. He understands his business and discharges his duties in a genial gentlemanly manner, and he has, right here, our acknowledgements for a most delightful afternoon at the "World's Fair."[53]

The show was larger than in the first two years. The 130 workmen of 1872 became 300 in 1873. The canvas crew was the largest section at eighty-eight men. The teamsters numbered forty-five, as did the train crew. Advertising, including the billposters, employed twenty. The menagerie crew had eighteen.

The number of tents on the lot was increasing for all of the major circuses. This was primarily due to the standard

for large pavilions set by the Barnum show in 1871. It served
as a measure of greatness—the larger the canvas spread, the
larger the circus on the inside. The advertisements listed
these numbers, as well as exaggerated claims of seating ca-
pacities. "10 tents cover 5 acres," and "Seven Superior Exhibitions, in Six Separate Colossal Tents," were the Barnum
boasts in 1872. Adam Forepaugh, a chief competitor, followed with "four enormous tents" and "118,558 square feet
of canvases" the same season. Two years later his ads read
"eight center pole tents, accommodating 10,000 spectators."
A Baltimore paper hit the nail on the head with: "Now each
showman brags of his expanse of canvas, and makes the
number of his tents an advertising card, while those who visit
the show find more tents about it than anything else, and a
show is scattered through six tents that would not transcend
the capacity of two."[54]

      Twenty-four tents were made for the Barnum show
this season, four of which were held in reserve. The big top
had three center poles, and sixty quarter-poles, probably a
200 foot round-top with two fifty foot middles, making it
300 by 200 feet, large enough for two rings and a hippodrome track. This is confirmed by an item in the Pittsburgh
Post which read: "Imagine an arena 300 x 200 feet, the center occupied by two large rings, and the outer space so judi-
ciously distributed in seats, rising one above the other, that
the performance in both circles can be enjoyed with equal
satisfaction."[55] The Baltimore *American and Commercial
Advertiser* echoed this with: "These take place in an adjoining tent, which is in the form of an immense oval, 300 by
200 feet ...."[56] As did the Titusville *Morning Herald*: "The
main museum was 1,000 feet in length and the circus tent
300 feet long, ... and two arenas, with an outer ring."[57] The
third ring, a track encircling the other two, was used exclusively for the "Grand Oriental Pageant" (grand entrée).[58]

Above: Barnum tent layout for 1873. Below: enlargement of the three center-pole main canvas. The photograph is the property of the Circus World Museum, Baraboo, Wisconsin.

Grand entrée sketch, showing 2 rings and a hippodrome track. Published in the 1873 P. T. Barnum Advance Courier.

Grand entrée sketch—2 rings and a hippodrome track—
at Barnum's circus, Fourth Avenue and Twenty-Seventh
Street, the site of the old New Haven Railroad depot,
where the show opened on November 20, 1873. Published in the New York *Daily Graphic*, October 28, 1873.

Sketch depicting P. T. Barnum's Greatest Show on Earth, including the grand endrée—2 rings and a hippodrome track. Published in the Rochester *Evening Express*, June 21, 1873.

The acts being performed in the two main rings simultaneously were impressively coordinated. Frank Whittaker, the experienced equestrian director sat near the entrance to the arena and directed the activity by the use of a small gong. There were no "splurgy" announcements to interfere with the progression of the program. And the clowns did not serve as a filler for prolonging the entertainment.[59]

The main tent now seated some 13,000. Oddly, there were only six ushers listed, who most likely worked the reserved seat section. The bleachers were described by the Boston *Globe* as "common seats of pine boards ... a little wider and a degree softer than associated with the idea of a circus," and the reserved seats in the upper circle were "comfortable enough for any one."[60] Comfort, of course, can always be equated with the enjoyment of the sitter.

The greatest innovation of the season was the adoption of the two ring configuration. The move was motivated by problems incurred from the enlargement of the canvas pavilion in 1872, which placed the end seating at a greater distance from the ring than seating on the sides. Because of this, spectators frequently left their places and moved to ringside for better viewing, which created a bothersome crowd control problem for management. The advent of this innovation has been related by Dan Castello: "Barnum came to me and asked what we were going to do, as the canvas was getting so big that the people could not see. I told him that we would have to put in two rings."[61] The upshot was that two groups of performers, as near alike as possible, duplicated each other in rings placed side by side, advertised as two circuses in one. The price of admission did not change for this "double show"—still 50¢ for adults; children under nine years of age, 25¢.

One unique addition to the lot layout was a 100 by 150 foot tent that was intended as an area for the public to rest while waiting for the performance to begin. When the front door opened the tent was closed. Several cages of animals and a sideshow attraction or two were placed there, and no admission was charged. This was alluded to in *Frank Leslie's Illustrated Weekly* at the outset of the season, when Barnum wrote:

> Among some of my novelties is a FREE FULL MENAGERIE OF WILD ANIMALS, including all, and more, than are usually seen in a traveling menagerie, which I now open to be seen by everybody, WITHOUT ANY CHARGE WHATEVER. The expense of these animals and of transporting these FREE TENTS through the country, all of which I exhibit absolutely FOR NOTHING, costs me as much as an ordinary menagerie for which other managers charge 50 cents admission.[62]

The enlarging of the tented arena and the construction time lost because of the three performance a day schedule required an advance crew of twenty men under the supervision of Charles McLean, who had come over from the Older show, to travel ahead of the company to prepare the lot (two to three acres). They built the ring banks, earthen rings used with wooden stakes atop them from which canvas curtains about two feet high were suspended. They leveled the ground for the hippodrome track on which spectacles were held.

Another Coup innovation, necessitated by performing in the larger cities, was the advance construction of additional seating in localities where increased attendance was expected. The workmen ahead of the show bought lumber from local merchants and pre-built wooden bleachers to augment the circus' movable seating. We learn that in Buffalo, two weeks before the show's arrival, workmen constructed a "raised gallery ... accessible by broad stairways" that provided an additional "three thousand sittings."[63] The

Cleveland *Plain Dealer* indicated that "in large cities like Cleveland an extra amphitheatre is erected, giving three thousand additional seats."[64] For the Pittsburgh engagement, the *Post* announced that carpenters were busily building "the grand wooden amphitheatre at Union Park, a structure which Mr. Barnum is obliged to erect in order to accommodate the multitudes that daily attend."[65] And a "grand wooden amphitheatre" was built on the lot at Broad and Diamond Streets for the Philadelphia engagement commencing September 29.[66] This technique was to be continued and expanded when Barnum's Great Roman Hippodrome was taken on the road in 1874 and 1875.

The circus program was one of the largest seen to this time. There were sixteen changes, all but three of them involving both rings—one ring was decorated blue, the other crimson—plus acts that appeared on the hippodrome track. Thus, though fifteen or sixteen separate acts had been the industry norm for twenty years, with Barnum this number was doubled in 1873.[67]

Where the Barnum show had a decided advantage was, as usual, in the museum. Under the direction of W. L. Jukes, the great constructor of automata, this department mirrored the intense nineteenth-century public interest in machinery carried to rather absurd lengths. There were "busy city" tableaus of Jupiter's palace, a Louis XVI hunting scene, the siege of Paris, the games of Olympus and the like. A portrait gallery of American presidents and internationally famous men (not a single woman) was featured. There were automaton bell ringers, a grotto of Calypso, the garden of the Hesperides, five hundred stuffed birds, some of which sang.

Professor Faber's talking machine (a disembodied head which seemed to speak) was a new attraction. The contraption sang, laughed, and talked in various languages. According to the advertisements, Barnum paid $20,000 for a six

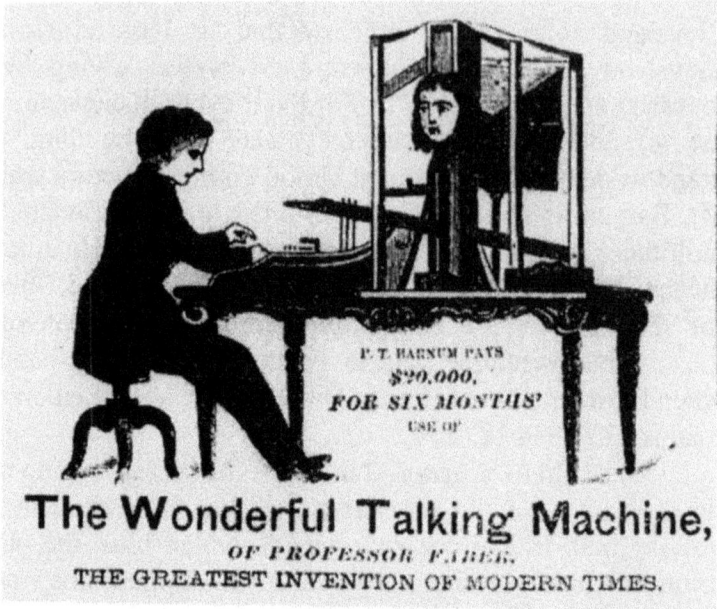

The Wonderful Talking Machine,
OF PROFESSOR FABER.
THE GREATEST INVENTION OF MODERN TIMES.

month exclusivity. "It assuredly talks plainer than its inventor," the Buffalo *Daily Courier* asserted, "and if it were properly stimulated to it, we can scarcely doubt that it would put the lady who manipulates the keys to a severe test."[68] The Titusville *Morning Herald* found the machine to be a true advancement of mechanical science: "We can hardly expect that the infant would speak as well as the full grown man; but the mechanism of this machine is but in its infancy, yet articulates words with remarkable modulation."[69]

Human curiosities were used to parade around the hippodrome track during the performance. These people were separate from the museum department, as it was known. Exhibited by S. S. Smith, the group consisted of the midget Admiral Dot; Charles Tripp, the armless boy; "Zip" (William H. Jackson) the "What is it?"; the Fiji Cannibals, and the cast of "Digger Indians." In addition to appearing on the track at the beginning of the performance, they occupied a separate tent (not to be confused with the Bunnell Brothers' sideshow), previously mentioned as a free pre-show area.[70]

Zalumma Agra, a Circassian lady, was also included in the group. It can be said that she and her genre were invented by Barnum. In 1864, in an attempt to perpetuate the myth that there was a breed of people, the purest and handsomest representatives of the Caucasian race, living in the mountains near the Black Sea, Barnum instructed an agent named John Greenwood, Jr., to seek out and return with a sample. "I still have faith in a beautiful Circassian girl if you can get one very beautiful," he wrote in a letter to Greenwood. He was willing to pay $4,000 or $5,000 in gold to buy one, "but it must be understood she is free ...."[71] Greenwood returned empty-handed, but within a short time America was introduced to the first of a string of fake beauties appearing as Circassians, found in the mountains of Manhattan near the East River. Coiffeured with frizzy hair and costumed as a Turk, she was introduced to New Yorkers as Zalumma Agra, the "Star of the East." Whether or not this Zalumma Agra of 1873 was the same specimen as 1864 is unknown to me. What is apparent, however, is that beneath the vapor of P. T.'s moral preachments there remained the same old humbuggery.

The menagerie, once it was recalled from P. A. Older's Barnum Show in New Orleans, and with new additions, was as extensive as any, and lacked only a hippopotamus of the larger beasts. There were two replacements for the four giraffes lost in the Hippotheatron fire, one of which was kept in reserve in Bridgeport against further loss. The rhinoceros had escaped death because he was with the Older circus at the time of the fire. There were four elephants, two of which, Gypsy and Betsy, performed. The caged animals

Zalumma Agra, the Circassian Beauty

occupied nearly thirty wagons. There were also live birds, from cassowaries to humming birds. And there were the usual lions, tigers, leopards, cheetahs, a polar bear, a wart hog, sea lions—all the "world in tribute," as the Advance Courier had it. A shipment of animals was added to the menagerie for its Pittsburgh stand at Union Park in Allegheny City on July 7-10. Included in the lot were four giraffes.

An original device this year was the use of the circus train to publicize the show. A new steam calliope, twenty-four feet long and seven feet wide, was played along the route as the train approached each city.[72] In union with its music, comic gymnastics were performed atop several cages by automaton figures furnished by Prof. J. L. Jukes. The train also included five sleeping cars and six passenger cars owned by the Barnum people.[73]

Circuses had been bedeviled in the past by petty thieves and other riffraff that followed them from place to place, preying on the people who attended performances. From the outset, the Barnum show had detectives on the payroll to patrol the lot and rid it of the unsavory element. But the increase in the size of tents at this time, with the capacity for seating more people, thereby bringing larger numbers to the exhibition grounds, multiplied the possibilities of nefarious behavior. Local newspapers warned their readers to be wary of buying spurious tickets hawked on the streets. "The ticket wagons are sufficiently numerous to supply the multitude on the shortest possible notice," a Boston paper gave assurance, "and from the regular ticket sellers the public should supply themselves." Leave your watches and jewelry at home and come to the circus with just the amount of money needed, was the warning against the epidemic of pickpockets.[73] "The pickpockets in the vicinity of the exhibition [were] kept shy [by] our own and Barnum's detectives," assured the Buffalo *Daily Courier*, "and at our present

writing we hear of only one pocket being relieved of its
pocket-book."[74]

The "Greatest Show on Earth" opened the season at
the former Empire Rink, now called the American Institute,
for two weeks beginning March 29. From a description in
the New York *Times* of April 4, we know that both rings
were used, with simultaneous performances in each. The
first date under canvas was at Brooklyn on April 16-19.
Following this, the show was loaded onto railroad cars and
began the touring season. The trains had sixty-two to sixty-
five cars of which fifty were Barnum's, the rest leased. The
variation in numbers had to do with the various sizes of the
cars provided by the individual railroads.

The route took the show into New England, across
New York state to Buffalo, through Ohio, into Indiana and
Illinois, coming up to Chicago, the furthest western point
reached. They played there for a week, then went into Michigan, across Ontario, down to Washington and Baltimore,
and a week in Philadelphia. Another week in Brooklyn
ended the tenting season. All the important cities in the
north were visited. There were week-long stands in St.
Louis, Chicago, Philadelphia and Brooklyn, ten days in
Boston, and four-day stops in Cincinnati and Baltimore.
Three shows were given each day, generally at 10 a.m., 1
p.m., and 7 p.m., the exact times being subject to rail con-
nections. 515 performances, plus or minus, were given, with
an average audience of nearly 9,700 at each, three times the
capacity of most circuses. The operation was so efficient
that only one performance was missed, the morning show in
Lafayette, Indiana, on July 30, caused by a railroad accident
ahead of the circus trains.

The immense size of the entire circus was overwhelming to the public, and Barnum, of course, was the first
to acknowledge it: "I have been enabled, through the aid of

cable dispatches, electricity and steam, and the expenditure of nearly a million of dollars, to place upon the road by far the largest and most interesting combination of Museum, Menagerie and Hippodrome ever known before—a veritable World's Fair."[75]   The Pittsburgh *Post* reported that the tent was the largest seen in that city, where on opening night 13,000 people attended the performance. "If Barnum's show in this city about a year ago was vast," the writer mused, "the present one should be classed as so superlatively colossal as almost to defy our catalogue of adjectives."[76]   The Battle Creek *Daily Journal* reiterated the image: "In every part of the mammoth tent there was a crowd, and when the performance began in the two rings there were but a few vacant seats in the vast range of benches which are prepared for the accommodation of fourteen thousand persons."[77]

Ben Lusbie was still in the main ticket wagon—receiving money, making change, and passing out tickets with his famous lightning speed. He was assisted by other sellers and in most cities they were sorely needed. For example, at Rochester, New York, where school children were released from their lessons and where the thoroughfares leading from the country had been jammed with traffic since the first ray of the sun, the afternoon entertainment packed upwards of 15,000 people into the big top, the crowd swelled by a large constituency that had been brought over in a steamer from Canada. There was an audience of an additional 10,000 for the night performance.

We can still see Barnum's presence in the advertising department. The familiar bywords of "moral" and "educational" were again in use and their cumulative effect from other seasons apparent, confirmed by a line from the Troy (NY) *Budget*: "The show goes about the country more as a missionary than as a mountebank, and sets a good example of sobriety and industry to everybody."[78]

While visiting the show at Cleveland in July, Barnum performed an humanitarian gesture that perhaps only he could accomplish. A seven year old boy of a Cleveland family, friends of Barnum, was recovering from a severe illness. His disappointment at not being able to enjoy the menagerie exhibition was made known to the showman. Whereupon, between the matinee and the evening performance, a caravan of the four elephants and all the camels and dromedaries appeared in front of the family home. With a large crowd gathered in the street and the lad watching from a window, the two trained elephants went through their various routines.[79] It can be readily assumed there were members of the press among the congregation.

At a time when circuses were chided for the numerous sideshows and booths that followed them from town to town, many that acquired the privilege of setting up on the show grounds, it is refreshing to read that on occasion there were established booths for charitable purposes. At Rochester, the ladies of St. Patrick's congregation were represented, where they sold articles for the benefit of the orphans. Such a privilege was given them by Barnum's treasurer, S. H. Hurd (who made a donation of $20 from his own pocket).[80]

The 1873 season exceeded the successes of the previous two, yet keeping to the Barnum philosophy of offering more for the money than any other show. The reaction of the public and the press was unprecedented.

At season's end, the circus moved onto the site of the former New Haven Railroad depot, between Madison and Fourth Avenues and 26th and 27th Streets, where a wooden seating amphitheatre was constructed. This was the only prime vacant site in the city which could accommodate a large spread of canvas. The *Clipper* announced that a series of new tents, "then erected for the first time," covered the

entire city block.[81] The menagerie occupied one half of the
main tent and the double circus the other. The advertising
suggests that the stand was not intended to be lengthy. "A
GRAND WOODEN AMPHITHEATRE, built expressly for this
occasion, in conjunction with the COLOSSAL HIPPODROME
PAVILIONS, enable the management to inaugurate one of the
most brilliant, though brief, seasons of equestro-zoological
pastimes ever presented to a metropolitan audiences." It
may be that the American Institute was not available until
late in November.

The New York *Times* asserted that an audience of
some 3,000 people crowded into what was "probably the
largest tent ever seen in this city," in spite of the stormy
weather that left the canvas dripping.[82] Damp or dry, the
audience, who were experiencing a two-ring performance for
the first time, were a bit thunderstruck. As was reported:
"The circuses formed a bewildering sight. To patiently gaze
upon the attractions of one alone was to lose sight of the
novel delights of the other, and the management's love of
colossal entertainments must be held chiefly responsible for
the unhappy feelings which seemed to pervade a large portion of the audience."[83] The crowds were so great at this
stand that it was necessary to enlarge the wooden amphitheatre. But one of the main attractions was not present.
Barnum had left for Europe in September, "looking for novelties." On November 19 his wife, Charity, died at their
home in Connecticut. Barnum, however, remained abroad
until the opening of his Great Roman Hippodrome in April.

After the run ended, the circus company moved in-
doors at the American Institute building at 63rd Street and
Third Avenue for a winter season, opening November 26 in a
venue that was heated by steam. Just as throughout the season, performances were given in two separate rings. A
spectacle involving a mock battle was staged for the Christ-

mas season; when soldiers on horse and foot stormed a
mimic fort amid roars from cannon and musketry; and, upon
victory, ran up the American flag to cheers from the audience.

Three years of triumphant tours! Undoubtedly the
most innovative three years of circus history in this country.
And to the outside world this was Barnum's show, attributed
to Barnum's genius. Through use of his personal notices in
the press, his columns in the advance couriers, and the thousands of copies of his autobiography, all devoted to "self-
puffery," he ingeniously elevated his already celebrated image to a new level. Journalists accepted the Barnum myth
and ardently propounded it. A testimonial in the Buffalo
Daily Courier is typical of innumerable newspaper voices
across the country: "We are not apt to associate the idea of
genius with managerial character. We are content to speak
of a manager's tact and energy if he shows these qualities;
but the term 'genius' can be applied to Mr. Barnum with all
the force and meaning it carries with it."[84]

But what of the labors of W. C. Coup? His three
years of circus management, undeniably successful, were
obscured by the Barnum image, a circumstance which Coup
had shrewdly foreseen and then, because it worked to his advantage, perpetuated to its fullest. Admittedly, success was
accomplished through Barnum's generous investments, his
extraordinary sense of what the public wanted in entertainment, and the incredible magic of the Barnum name. Because of this some people have cast doubt on Coup's ability,
bolstered by his failures in later years, but which occurred
under vastly different circumstances. It cannot be denied
that under Coup's management the gross income expanded
two and a half times in 1872, and fifty per-cent above that in
1873 ($1.5 million versus $1 million). One cannot overlook
his innovations, his organizational ability, and his efficiency

in management. As we now leave Coup behind in the advancement of our narrative, we gladly lift our hat to him, a man who brought the Barnum name to the circus world and with it created a new era for traveling entertainments.

GREAT LONDON SHOW.
WE DO THIS AS REPRESENTED
Will open at GILMORE'S GARDEN OCTOBER 22nd

II
THE SAGA OF HOWES'
GREAT LONDON

NOTHER CIRCUS WAS INTRODUCED to American audiences in 1871, one that would play an important role in the genealogical progression toward the marriage of Barnum and Bailey. It was called Howes' Great London Circus and Sanger's English Menagerie. The founder was the wealthy and experienced showman, Seth B. Howes.[1]

Howes has been called the "Father of the American Circus." He was one of those Putnam County, New York, natives who entered the field early, made his mark, and prospered. Young Seth's choice of profession was most likely influenced by his much older brother, Nathan A., who preceded him in the circus business. In his *Annals of the American Circus*, Stuart Thayer first lists Master Seth B. Howes, rider, with a small troupe under the management of Nathan Howes, Aaron Turner, and Sylvester Reynolds in 1826. Seth continued to work for Nathan for several years as assistant manager, equestrian director, and ringmaster.[2]

In 1841, Nathan entered into partnership with E. F. and J. Mabie and installed Seth as manager of the New York Circus, sometimes advertised as the Olympic Circus. The next year Nathan took over the management and relegated Seth to equestrian director. Then, in 1843, Seth and E. F. Mabie were listed as managers and proprietors. This lasted through 1846 when Seth sold his interest and organized S. B. Howes & Co., which he operated for the next three seasons.

Seth Howes' partnership with Barnum and Sherwood Stratton in 1851, forming P. T. Barnum's Asiatic Caravan, Museum and Menagerie, is related earlier. Two years later he was part of a group—Richard Sands, John J. Nathans, and Avery Smith—that brought Franconi's Hippodrome to New York City. The men acquired the costumes and equipment formerly belonging to William Batty's Grand National Hippodrome, which had been prepared for the Great London Exposition of 1851. A company of European artists was assembled, headed by Madame and Henri Franconi and augmented by American performers from Sands, Quick & Co.'s circus. In addition to the Franconi establishment in New York City, a road unit was formed under the Franconi title which toured for the seasons of 1853 and 1854, managed by Joseph Chiarini.

Then, in 1857, Seth Howes took another important step by transporting a circus to Europe. In association with Joe Cushing, the venture under the title of Howes & Cushing's Great American Circus and Menagerie met with immediate success. For a time there were two companies under canvas. Shortly after opening at the Alhambra Palace, London, the performance of May 14, 1858, was attended by the Queen, the Prince Consort, the Royal Family and court.[3]

During this engagement abroad, on January 26, 1861, Seth took an English wife. The bride was Miss Amy Moseley, a nineteen year old equestrienne, who, according to C. G. Sturtevant, was the daughter of a London merchant.[4] She was a lady of intelligence and taste, who was said to have been a major influence in the artistic selections relating to pageant wagons and other parade and show elements within the Howes organization.

After seven years abroad, Howes made a triumphant return to the United States when in 1864 he took Avery Smith, Gerard C. Quick, and John J. Nathans as partners for a show that went out as S. B. Howes' Great European Circus. Considered to be one of the largest and finest aggregations on the road, it carried impressive parade flash, particularly an elegant display of numerous English pageant wagons.

James Crockett and Sanger's den of six performing lions, an act that had been contracted in England and had accompanied Howes to America, was a featured attraction. Crockett, born in Preston, England, the son of a circus musician, was following his father's calling as a member of Sanger's band before he was forced to abandon the sharps and flats of the profession because of weakened lungs. As it happened, Sanger had bought five lions at that time but had no one to perform them until Crockett volunteered, his only attributes being an imposing stature and youthful impulse. But he proved himself to be a man of great nerve and unwavering courage and was soon performing the feats of Van Amburgh and Carter and traveling around Great Britain and the European continent, winning plaudits and receiving gifts from royalty.

Managed by Avery Smith, Howes' Great European opened in Detroit on May 9, 1864. Following the Michigan stands, the wagon show toured in Indiana, Illinois, Wisconsin, and Iowa. It then re-organized in St. Louis under the management of John J. Nathans and worked south, performing in Memphis and Vicksburg and on to New Orleans for a winter engagement. The following year Howes went into semi-retirement when he sold his share to his partners, who continued operation through 1871.

    Howes returned to England in 1870, leaving February 2 on the steamer *Iris* with his twin nephews, Egbert and Elbert, sons of his brother Nathan. He landed at Liverpool on March 19, after an absence of seven years, and set about organizing a show. In a letter to P. T. Barnum some years later, he wrote that he intended a tour of Europe; but the idea was abandoned because of the Franco-Prussian War. As a result, the company confined its performances to England, and then only for a season.

    Similar to his earlier visit abroad, he made deals with Lord George Sanger for a collection of rare animals and ornate pageant wagons. Even so, according to an advertisement, he brought with him a number of curious and rare animals, including a drove of camels and dromedaries. One of the parade features was the "Car of Juggernaut" on which was mounted a "magnificently caparisoned idol image elephant."

Another advertised feature was the American, Charles Herman, and his pack of performing wolves and bears, an act never before witnessed on the British Isles. The wolves, it was claimed, were trained to "tear raw meat from a girdle" tied around Herman's neck. There was also M. Ollivier and his celebrated performing monkeys, which had met with success at the Holborn Amphitheatre the previous winter. A number of English and European performers were engaged, the handbill listing riders James and Marie Jee and Miss Clara Rice, and an act called the American Brothers, composed of men who made flying leaps over horses, ponies, and camels.

It was suggested by Lord Sanger's agent, Harry Montague, that competition from the Sanger circus drove Howes out of the country. His explanation was that two large tented outfits could not survive in such limited territory. The Sanger people, representing the foremost concern of its kind on the British Isles, were determined to eliminate the Yankee interloper. This was done by billing all of the towns along the route a day in advance of Howes' arrival, it being known that English audiences were accustomed to waiting to attend the last show to arrive when two or more were advertised at the same time and place. In addition, the Sanger outfit went into the northern towns well in advance of, and uncontested by, their adversary. Finally, the two shows played day-and-date in Preston, Lancashire, bringing the American company to the realization that the fight was lost and necessitating a return to the United States.[4]

One must be suspicious of Montague's claims. As Sanger's agent he cannot be looked upon as an unbiased observer; but, rather, one who would benefit by exaggerated accomplishments. Rivalry, however, was an expected element of the business and rivalry between the two shows no doubt occurred. Still, Howes had friendly business dealings with Sanger in buying the parade wagons and the menagerie animals; and before leaving, Sanger and Howes made a deal which would enrich the English manager £2,000 a year for the use of his name.[5]

A final chapter to the tour was the Bristol stand which began on October 17. While there the circus encountered rebellion from members of the audience, a serious situation created by an unexpectedly large turnout for the evening performance. The management had issued more tickets than there were seats, which caused a spilling over of audience members into the ring, making it impossible to proceed with some of the acts. The performers continued as best they could until 9:30 p.m., at which time the band played the national anthem to conclude the program. Some of the audience members, feeling they had been deprived of the full entertainment, actively expressed their resentment. Stones were thrown at the lamps illuminating the arena with effective accuracy. A mob outside the tent entered from underneath the sidewall to join the melee by pelting the circus people with stones. Others drew knives and set about doing great damage to the canvas. The disturbance was finally quieted by a detachment of constables summoned from the Central Police Station. The proprietors, fearing more trouble and benefiting from improved judgment, left town after the following matinee. Shortly, the animals, chariots, personnel, and some circus paraphernalia were shipped across the Atlantic in time to open an 1871 summer season in the United States.

Early in his career Howes was a large investor in Chicago real estate. At one time he owned a tract covering over 1,000 acres in a suburban part of the city where Hyde Park is now located. After selling a portion of it, he purchased property within the city and made it highly income producing, a move that established him as one of the most wealthiest of American circus proprietors. So, eager to enjoy the benefits of his riches, at age fifty-six, he was prepared to retire and turn the circus of his name over to nephews Egbert and Elbert.

Egbert Howes assumed the management of the Great London. As a youngster, he had traveled with his father's circuses and in 1857, as a young man, went to the British Isles with Uncle Seth. At times during the visit to England, Ireland, Scotland and Wales he managed the show. In 1859 he married equestrienne Jennie Maude Jee, a member of a famous British circus family. After returning to the United States, he was treasurer and part owner of the Nixon/Castello circus in 1868; and manager during its famous trans-continental tour to the Pacific coast in 1869.

Elbert Howes also traveled with his father's circuses, and later went to England with uncle Seth. Although he was not involved directly in circus management, he was active in the procurement of exotic animals for the concern. During a trip to Ceylon, he acquired some of the finest elephants ever exhibited. But unlike Egbert, who remained active in the circus until his death, Elbert's show life ended when James E. Kelly and Henry Barnum took over the Great London following the 1872 season. He then settled in Brewster, New York, and focused his attention on politics, occupying a five year position of town supervisor and, following that, gate keeper of the Drewville Reservoir.

Howes' Great London Circus and Sanger's English Menagerie was advertised in 1871 as the only English equestrian institution in the United States—English riders, acrobats, and gymnasts.[6] The equipage was costly and magnificent, the horses well conditioned, the wild animal performances rare and varied, the arenic artist new to this country,

the drollery of the clowns unique to the audiences, and the
street procession the finest on the road.

In addition to the Sanger menagerie stock, Howes
had acquired animals trained to perform. There were four
trick ponies and six zebras that worked in harness. What
seems to be a unique act at this time was a pack of hyenas
exhibited by a Signor Delhi Montano, who was billed as a
cannibal Hottentot. An Italian tamer of wild beasts, Moloch
the Invincible, performed five royal Bengal tigers, wrestling
and tossing them "like so many kittens, without the slightest
appreciation of personal consequences."[7]

The menagerie collection included a gnu, a red stag
of India, a west African lion, a sable antelope, long horned
elands, spotted Jerusalem donkeys, and a cage of monkeys.
There were also macaws, parrots, parakeets, ostriches, a king
vulture, a bird of paradise, and a crested jet black cassowary.
Advance notices boasted of sixteen performing ponies, sixty
Flemish horses, a team of eight spotted donkeys, and a bri-
dled gnu.

An advertisement announced that the show would arrive at Oshawa, Ontario, on August 17 with a number of elephants as part of the company. We know that Elbert Howes had been sent from Europe to Ceylon in 1870 to purchase them. During his sojourn he acquired eleven, but one died aboard ship en route to the United States. The return voyage from Ceylon, which took four months, was depicted by the ship's skipper, Capt. Smalley, for the New York *Times*.

According to Smalley, the elephants were trapped in the jungles of the Mannah District and all but one were "fresh caught and wild." On the face of it, this sounds questionable. All elephants have to go through a process of domestication before being transplanted into a civilized setting, trained to obedience by handlers and the performance of at least the simplest of work assignments. In all probability, what Capt. Smalley meant was that the professional middlemen were bypassed and Howes went directly to the natives who captured and trained the animals.

The purchased elephants were loaded onto the boat at Colombo, Ceylon, by means of canvas slings, with ropes and pulleys attached to the rigging and mainsail boom. Forty-five natives were employed in the hoisting and lowering process. Once on board the elephants were stowed between decks where stalls had been built of teak wood strong enough to resist pressure of 2,000 pounds and so arranged as to safely keep each elephant in place and separated from the others in the roughest of weather.[8]

The ten elephants arrived at the New York City docks at the foot of Thirteenth Street on July 22, 1871, aboard the *Nehemiah Gibson*. They were lodged overnight in the Eleventh Avenue stables of the Hudson River Railroad; then, in the morning of the 23rd, they were walked to the depot by their Singhalese keepers and boarded onto five large produce cars for shipment to their circus homes.[9]

Two of the elephants went to Van Amburgh's Great Golden Menagerie at Joliet, Illinois, joining on July 29. The remaining eight were sent north to Howes' Great London, then in Canada.[10] The earliest indication of elephants with the Howes circus came in an advertisement in the Oshawa *Vindicator* of August 2 which announced that a herd of ten elephants—ten—had just arrived and would appear in the procession harnessed to the "Car of Juggernaut," the great war elephant Rajah being among them. The Toronto *Daily Telegram* of August 7 merely included the simple line, "the herd of elephants."[11] On the 11th, information in the Ontario *Reformer* was a repeat of what had been published in the Oshawa *Vindicator*. A pre-appearance reader in the same paper, promoting the exhibition in Oshawa on the 17th, included the following: "Since the arrival of the troupe in Canada, they have received by an arrival from the East Indies ten Asiatic elephants, which will appear in the grand procession into town, harnessed to one of their Colossal Chariots."[12] Ten elephants! The inference suggests that all ten elephants joined Howes' Great London in Canada, which is plausible. The ten could have been shipped there, after which two were then sent on to the Van Amburgh show in Illinois. It is hard to imagine that the two elephants, which were said to have boarded a railroad car on July 23 would be in transit until the 29th. If they did join the Howes circus first, the arrival of the full ten may have received advance publicity before the decision was made when to ship the animals south to the Van Amburgh show. An ad for an Elmira, New York, appearance of October 10 includes, "A herd of eight elephants will lead the entrance of the companies into this city." The names of the eight were listed as Rajah, Mandarin, Hannibal, Bismark, Mercury, Utopia, Victoria, and the baby elephant

Princess. Despite all of the confusion, this group of elephants joining Howes' Great London constituted the largest herd toured by a show since the P. T. Barnum's Asiatic Caravan, Museum and Menagerie went on the road in 1851.

The shipment from Ceylon was reportedly consigned to Van Amburgh menagerie proprietor, James E. Kelly. If this is true, we can only speculate that Kelly financed Elbert Howes' trip and was the purchaser of the elephants. We know that he had an interest in the Howes' Great London from its outset. It may be that his elephants represented that investment.

The Howes street procession was particularly enlivened by the imported golden chariots. The "War Chariot of India, or Car of Juggernaut," as in the previous year in England, was surmounted by a life-sized golden idol elephant, surrounded by Turks, Moors, Sultans, etc. The "Golden Chariot of Commerce," made to raise and lower a telescopic portion by machinery, was covered with heavy carvings and richly gilded ornaments. On pedestals in the rear were statues of Britannia and Columbia, representing Europe and America. The "Golden Chariot of Euterpe" was a bandwagon with French plate mirrors on the side in bas-relief, representing all nations. The "Golden Dragon Chariot," symbolizing Egypt, was decorated with a fiery three-headed dragon. The "Celestial Golden Chariot," surmounted by a canopy the entire length, draped with red, white, blue, and gold, paid tribute to China. Lastly, for the benefit of children, there was the "Fairy Cinderella Chariot."

These were the heart and soul of the procession. According to a pre-season announcement, the event was to be lead by four heralds in full armor, mounted, carrying banners and trumpets, and followed in order by: the "Car of Euterpe" drawn by ten Flemish horses and carrying Emidy's British

Band; the Chariot of Commerce; the Egyptian Dragon Chariot drawn by eight donkeys; a caravan of eight wild animal
cages, twenty Roman horsemen in full armor; Moors, Turks,
and Arabs, attended by a band of Amazons in full armor; the
Cinderella Fairy Chariot, drawn by Lilliputian piebald ponies; a Chinese palanquin, constructed of wickerwork, drawn
by six zebras in harness; a cavalcade of twenty armed
knights; and, bringing up the rear, the War Chariot of India,
or Car of Juggernaut, drawn by a number of elephants.[13]
This ensemble of pageantry was the largest and most grand
of all the shows on the road.

     The ring performance and the menagerie shared a
single tent. It was brilliantly lighted by the Patent Maxim
Gas Machine, which was fed by flexible hoses. The system
allowed free ventilation throughout the pavilion.

     It was advertised that the names of the artists were all
new to the public, none of whom having ever appeared in
this country before. But the arenic program was solid and
may have out-classed Barnum's. James Jee, billed as the
only person to accomplish the forward feet-to-feet somersault on a bareback horse, was the featured rider. His sister,
Jennie, the young lady Egbert Howes had married in England in 1859, was an accomplished equestrienne. David Ab-
bey Seal performed as the principal clown and aerial leaper.
William Jee, another of the famous family, was a gymnast
and tumbling clown. And filling out a trio of jesters was the
Italian, Gabriel Almonte. Mr. L. Joseph performed dramatic
scenes on horseback, one being "The Ship-Wrecked Sailor
Boy." Faust and Ector displayed gymnastic powers of
strength and endurance; and the LeClair Brothers, John and
Shed (Shedrick Smith) worked the double trapeze. Lizzie
Keys, wife of David Seal, was the leading female rider, sup-
ported by two Jees, Mlle. Marie and Mlle. Alice, billed as
"European celebrities."

An incite regarding the company members can be found in the reminiscences of a Mr. A. Pember, who described himself as an "Amateur Vagabond." He discovered, after joining the company in Pawtucket, Rhode Island, that the ladies and gentlemen were quiet and reserved in manner; that "they would not tolerate for one moment companionship of anyone against whom there was a breath of suspicion." The dress of the lady riders was neat and tasteful, yet pretty and attractive, only short enough to enable them to go through their acts, and free from all unnecessary exposure of the shoulders and bosom. Nearly all were wives or husbands of members of the troupe; the equestrian Jee family being comprised of two brothers, the wife of one of the brothers, and three sisters.[14]

After single days in Mott Haven, Harlem, and Yorkville, the company made its American debut at the Sixty-Third Street Rink in New York City. According to the *Clipper*, the tent was erected inside the building. The New York *Times* reported that on the opening night the place hosted one of the largest audiences ever gathered there.[15] At the termination of the Rink engagement, the show followed a route around New York state, a territory that was already over-crowded with circuses.

The season ended on a note of tragedy. The band chariot with an eight-horse hitch met with disaster near Millerton, New York, on October 30. The driver lost control of it when the horses "spooked" while climbing a steep grade. When one of them stumbled to the ground the chariot veered off the road and over a steep embankment. Of the five musician passengers, two were crushed to death by the tumbling vehicle. Operations were disbanded the following day, blowing what would have been the last date in Millerton.

This might be seen as an omen. The Howes' Great London was a bad luck show. Although the title would persist for another seven years through three management teams, it would be, as Richard E. Conover suggested, "just one step ahead of the sheriff for most of its existence."[16]

The show organized at Brewster Station for the 1872 season and then went into the New England States. It consisted of 187 employees, 266 horses, and all moving on seventy-three wagons. The entire outfit was much the same as the previous year.[17] An exception, a most exciting addition to the program, was the trained elephant act. The eight-elephant herd of 1871 was cut to five, and at winter quarters they were taught to do some impressive feats, not the least of which was a five-animal pyramid. This remarkable pachyderm quintet, composed of Chieftain, Emperor, Sultan, Mandarin (sometimes shortened to Mandrie), and Victoria, remained as an act for many years thereafter.

The trainer was Stuart Craven, the greatest elephant man of his day. A native of Wooster, Ohio, Craven first appeared with the Van Amburgh show in 1857, where he broke and trained Tip Osage. The elephant was schooled to hold a perch while Craven climbed to its back and performed gymnastics. He also stood on its trunk and juggled as the beast ran around the ring. With the Mabie circus in 1859 he conquered Canada, later known as Romeo, one of the fieriest of beasts. He also worked for John O'Brien and Adam Forepaugh before leaving for Europe in 1867.

It was some years before Craven was acknowledged as the trainer of the Howes elephants. The first Great London advertisement we have found that included Craven's name was from a Fond du Lac, Wisconsin, newspaper announcing the show's arrival on August 12, 1875: "Only group of five performing elephants in the world ... all performing in the ring at the same time, just as represented on bills, programmes, &c. Trained and performed by Prof. Craven." It was confirmed later in a St. Louis *Globe-Dispatch* interview, in which he stated: "The next lot I trained were the five London elephants. I trained them when with the London show nine or ten years ago."[18] There was no one else around who could accomplish as much in so short a time. Remember, these elephants were barely out of the Ceylon jungle when they arrived in mid-summer of 1871. We speculate that Craven was with the show in the winter quarters of 1871-72 and may have remained with it until the end of the 1875 season, when he was replaced by George Arstingstall.

Howes' interest in the Great London was sold at the end of the 1872 season. Perhaps, as a Lockport, New York, correspondent reported, the performance was "too English" to suit local tastes.[19] But more to the point, competition had stiffened. With the Barnum show expanding to rail travel and other shows following, keeping in step required more funds than was available to the proprietors. The great Chicago fire that had occurred in October of 1871, destroying or damaging nearly one third of the total area, included valuable real estate owned by Seth B. He suffered heavy losses and his money was needed for rebuilding.

In spite of only two years of operation, the Great London under the Howes banner left an indelible imprint on the operation of circuses in America. As in 1864 with the Great European, the introduction of the numerous English pageant and parade wagons enlivened the processional aspect of shows for years to come. Add to this, the importation of the herd of ten elephants in 1871, and the featured act of five of them, initiated well over a decade of intense elephant competition in circus promotion and advertising. These elaborate wagons and the quintet of educated elephants will become a part of the Cooper & Bailey circus that in 1880 outclassed Mr. Barnum's show and forced him to seek a merger.

&

Howes' Great London went out under new ownership in 1873 after the majority of interest was sold to James E. Kelly following the 1872 season. Kelly was another one of those Putnam County men who had a talent for money. After leaving school he went into the banking business with Drew, Robinson & Co. on Wall Street and remained with that house for several years, even marrying the daughter of Daniel Drew. He later became a prosperous banker in his home town of Brewster, New York. Before putting money in Howes' Great London, he was connected with the Van Amburgh organization when, in 1861, he bought C. W. Gregory's holdings in the show and held them until the property was split up among the four proprietors.

There were two units on the road in 1871—Van Amburgh & Co.'s Great Golden Menagerie and Van Amburgh & Co.'s Mammoth Menagerie. The former, out of Brewster, New York, was managed by Henry Barnum; the latter, out of Connersville, Indiana, by Hyatt Frost. The four owners were James E. Kelly, Hyatt Frost, Henry Barnum, and O. J. Ferguson. At the end of the 1871 season the show ownership was divided, with Frost and Ferguson receiving the Connersville unit, as well as the rights to the Van Amburgh title. Kelly and Barnum took the other show which they based in Amenia, New York. This was toured in 1872 and 1873 as the Central Park Menagerie under Henry Barnum's management.

The Howes' Great London circus changed very little throughout its eight year existence under the three different managements. The elaborate English parade wagons and the five trained elephants remained the show's entertainment staple. R. H. and Elise Dockill were the backbone of the arenic acts from the time of their joining in 1873 until the show's closing in 1878. The other performers that came and went over those years provided the talent that kept the ring entertainment in line with the other leading circuses. The parade spectacle generally outclassed its competitors. The menagerie, particularly after it was combined with the Central Park show, was as good as most. And local newspaper responses were positive:

> The exhibition of Howes' Great London Circus is the best ever offered to the patronage of the public. Every portion of the exhibition is promptly and neatly done, and no word or action would offend the most refined and fastisdious.[20]

Yes, the performances were well appreciated by local audiences. The outfit was attractive. The show was competitively advertised. The ultimate "bugaboo," as we will see later, was Kelly's personal financial problems.

The 1873 company started out from Brewster Station, New York, with no apparent organizational changes from the previous year. Egbert Howes was retained as manager and Capt. Thomas Christopher as treasurer, both still having some financial interest in the show.[21] John Parks and Frank Uffner had the sideshow, concert, and candy privileges. The family of performing Jees were replaced by a strong company that featured the Dockrills.[22] Still an overland circus, the pre-season roster in the *Clipper* showed an inventory of 329 horses, 74 wagons, and some sixteen cages in the menagerie.

The show under the Howes management had remained in the East, but under the new proprietors it would soon become identified as a Middle West outfit. After a

short stay in New York state, the show moved into New
Jersey, Maryland, Virginia, and then Pennsylvania. Most
of the remainder of the season was devoted to Ohio and
Indiana, before closing and wintering at Connersville.

At the beginning of April, 1874, a train of forty-three
cars left Brewster Station for the Great London winter quarters with the Central Park Menagerie, Zoological Combination and Den Stone's Circus for a consolidation that would
add strength to the company. Henry Barnum, who by the
merging of the two shows acquired an interest in the Great
London, replaced Egbert Howes as general manager.

Barnum, a Bridgeport native, was a distant relative to
the great P. T. He had been involved in the circus business
since 1856, the better part of which was with the Van Amburgh organization. And now, although owning merely one-
tenth of Howes' Great London, the show was able to issue
advertising with prominently displayed headings that deceptively read: "Barnum & Co.'s Grand Central Park Menagerie
Consolidated for the Season of 1874 with Howes' Great
London Circus," much to the chagrin of the renowned Phineas Taylor.

The *Clipper's* pre-season 1874 roster listed twenty-
three tents on the lot and a compliment of 320 people.
George Coup was proprietor of the sideshow, which offered
the Madagascar Family, Circassian beauties, giants, dwarfs,
and a collection of mechanical wonders. John J. Parks and
Homer Davis, a duo who will play an even larger role later,
had the concert and candy privileges.

The show started out from Connersville on April 21,
and spent most of the season in Indiana and Michigan. From
the Jackson *Daily Citizen's* account of the show's visit to
that city, we know that the company arrived along the new
Napoleon road from Manchester, where it had set up the day
before. By 9:00 a.m. the tents were in the air, the crowds had

MME·ELISE·DOCKRILL·

R. H. Dockrill

formed, and the procession began along the streets of the city. The newspaper acknowledged that it was "the finest and most complete pageant which [had] ever preceded any circus that ever visited Jackson." There were those splendid gilded and mirrored chariot wagons, twenty-four ornate animal cages, a file of ladies and gentlemen, afoot and astride, a troupe of eleven mounted Iroquois Indians, five elephants, a number of ponies, and other attractions to appeal to the watchful sidewalk population massed along the route.[23]

1875 is the year the show took to rail travel. According to the St. Joseph *Gazette*, it was moved on forty-one cars and two locomotives. The transportation switch not only facilitated longer jumps but, as the Des Moines *Register* put it, it avoided "the dust and soil of the turnpike." This was particularly important to a circus that greatly relied on its magnificent street procession for creating local interest (the Janesville, Wisconsin, *City Times* reported it to be the best that had been exhibited there in years) and, therefore with need to protect the parade wagons from wear and tear and the grime that rough roads produced. And indeed the procession was still the big attraction.

> The procession eclipsed anything ever before seen in the capital of Iowa. The chariots appear like mountains of gold, and, seen when burnished by the bright sun, as yesterday, made a strikingly beautiful appearance. Wonderfully artistic work was done in their formation. Gilding and sculpture are alike marvels of beauty.[24]

In addition to the strong street show, there was heavy reliance on the performing animals. The by-now-famous five pyramid-forming elephants were advertised as trained and exhibited by Stuart Craven.[25] Five of the eight tigers were used in the ring; the other three were very young, said to be the first to be born in an American traveling menagerie

(born April 21, 1875). There was also the only five performing hyenas in the country.

> The animals of Mr. Sanger are unusually fine specimens, large,
> healthy, with no trace of the half-domesticated appearance that so
> much distracts from the interest of many similar exhibitions. Among
> them are a matronly tigress with a litter of three tiger cats. This sin-
> gle cage is worth the price of a ticket. There are five elephants, and
> all are trained. The pictured portrayed a pyramid of elephants, and, of
> course, everybody thought it was but a picture; inside was the reali-
> zation. The elephants formed the pyramid, just as represented. It was
> no sham, no humbug. Whatever the bill promised was fulfilled. A
> man or woman that attends Howe's circus, will get value received.[26]

The Kansas City *Journal of Commerce* assured its
readers that the show performance exceeded what was displayed on the bills:

> The animals are choice, numerous and interesting to look upon, while
> the entertainment throughout is certainly the best that has ever visited
> the West. The street parade itself forms an exhibition that is much
> better than one half the circus entertainments that have visited us. The
> chariots, the grand arrangements throughout, when formed in line,
> present a scene of grandeur such as one sees but once in a life time.[27]

The St. Joseph *Daily Morning Herald* complimented
the company on the courtesy of its staff and on it being a
place where one could take the whole family with certainty
that no disagreeable incident would occur, with no roughs,
thieves nor gamblers around the grounds.

Within a few years much will be made of the birth of
an elephant, said to the first to be born in captivity since the
days of the Roman Empire. Cooper, Bailey & Co.'s thousands of sheets of advertising will induce an enormous public curiosity in the event. To this day it is generally accepted
that indeed their baby elephant was the first to be born, not
only in the United States but in the entire Western World. I
am indebted to circus historian Richard J. Reynolds III for

calling my attention to an earlier incident of this phenomenon. In truth, an elephant was born at St. Joseph, Missouri,
when in 1875 the Howes' Great London circus was exhibiting in the West.

After the company had played Omaha, Nebraska, on
Saturday, May 29, and was using the Sunday lay-off to reach
their next stand of Kansas City, a female elephant became
sick, presumably from labor. The train was stopped at St.
Joseph, where she was taken off before the company continued on to their destination. The following day, Monday,
May 31, she gave birth. A short item in the St. Joseph *Daily
Morning Herald* of Tuesday, June 2, announced this unique
event:

> St. Joseph has the honor of having born within its limits the first baby
> elephant ever born in the United States. On Sunday, as Howes' cir-
> cus passed down the road, an elephantess became sick, and was put
> off at the Exposition Grounds. On Monday a young elephant put in
> an appearance, looking very much like its maternal ancestor. All day
> yesterday crowds flocked down to see the wee chap, and the prob-
> ability is they will increase in number today. Tomorrow the ele-
> phantess and her baby will be exhibited at the Great Circus and Me-
> nagerie.[28]

The next morning two more items appear in the paper, both on page one. A brief suggestion was offered within
a column titled City Condensed: "Would not St. Joseph be a
good name to give to the baby elephant born at the Exposition grounds in this city?" The second was a card bearing
the signature of Henry Barnum:

> THE BABY ELEPHANT
> It is Named in Honor of St. Joseph.
> The Mammoth Exhibition of the Age.
> Special to the *Morning Herald*, Atchison, Kas., June 2, 1875. Hon.
> John L. Bittinger:–Kiss the baby for me. I have named it "Joe," in
> honor of fair St. Joseph.

The New York *Clipper* confirmed the birth on June 12 in a short item that simply read: "A baby elephant was ushered into the world at St. Joseph, Mo., on May 31. Its mother travels with Howe's London Circus."

The circus was at the Kansas towns of Leavenworth on June 1 and Atchison on June 2, then returned to St. Joseph for a regularly scheduled date there on June 3, where the mother and calf were to be reunited with the show and supposedly put on display in the menagerie. Unfortunately, end of story.

There were no further acknowledgements of a baby elephant. In the account of the show's performance at St. Joseph, the *Daily Morning Herald*, noting that there was but a single omission in the program, stated, "Instead of five performing elephants there was but four—the fifth was taken sick on Monday last, and left at the Exposition grounds."[29] The only follow-up in the *Clipper* read: "The elephant, with Howes' London Circus, which had been ill, has recovered and rejoined the show, which is billed to exhibit as follows...." The entry ends with a list of dates to be played.[30]

What happened? Was the baby elephant a hoax? If it was a fraudulent birth, Reynolds asks, why pick St. Joseph, "It would be hard to sneak a calf into that town; the folks at the express office/depot would surely have spread the word of a baby elephant's arrival." It would make no business sense, he concluded, to debut it in a town the size of St. Joseph when there was much more to be gained by an unveiling in one of the more populated places.[31] If the purpose was to publicize the show, why were there no attempts after the initial birth announcements? This "first birth" received no ballyhoo from any quarter, indeed no follow-up of any kind. The only conclusion to be made is that the baby existed but did not survive more than a day. But why, with so much local excitement about the birth, was there no mention in the

Daily Morning Herald of the death? We regret we do not have the answer.

Thanks to rail transportation the 1875 itinerary was expansive. The show traveled from their Louisville winter quarters, where they open April 30, into Indiana, Illinois, Iowa, Kansas, Missouri, Minnesota, Wisconsin, Tennessee, Georgia, North and South Carolina.[32] The season closed at Dennison, Texas, on January 8 and the outfit was shipped to the Fair Grounds in St. Louis for the remainder of the winter.

If the season of 1875 was not good for circuses, 1876 was no better. The Chicago *Inter-Ocean* reported that the "panicky fever has overtaken circuses as well as other men and things." Accordingly, not a few "have 'burst up' this season, and only the more rigorous and substantial institutions have been able to weather the hard times."[33]

This year, 1876, the show claimed to move on forty-two railroad cars. There were twenty-two flats, ten palace horse cars, two palace elephant cars, four box cars, one baggage car, two palace sleeping cars, and one palace passenger car. The advertising assured the public that detectives were carried with the show and that everything about the organization was conducted in a most orderly manner. There was no gambling on the grounds, no monte playing or anything else. The 1,200 cushioned reserved seats formed a part of the total seating of approximately 5,000. The parade featured what was called a Mardi Gras Carnival, a commemorative spectacle in celebration of the centennial year, in which a number of maskers roistered to the music of the band. Along with the large assortment of animals, the elaborate, imported chariots still drew gasps from the curb watchers.

George Arstingstall, the elephant trainer, appears on the Howes' Great London roster for the first time. He was one of the top men in his field, perhaps second only to Stuart

Craven. Just prior to the Civil War he joined Dan Rice as an inexperienced animal man to work with bears. In 1866 he was with the Lipman circus handling a "sacred bull." A few years later he began making hot air balloon ascensions, but after falling some sixty-eight feet on one occasion, he decided training animals was a much safer profession. The few years before joining the Great London were spent in Europe working with a variety of animals.

The menagerie was respectable with about twenty cages. The elephant herd now numbered ten. The five performers—Chieftan, Emperor, Mandie, Sultan, and Victoria—stood on their heads, danced a jig on one foot, climbed ladders, and stood on tubs. The four Bengal tigers were handled by Herr Still.

The show continued to please. The Evansville, Indiana, *Daily Journal* called it by far the best circus ever given in that city, with a street procession that was the longest and most brilliant ever seen there. "The ordinary attractions of the Great London would be shining stars in any other circus," it stated. "They deserve the fullest meed (sic) of success wherever they go, and will, no doubt, get it all."[35] An item in the Chicago *Inter-Ocean* was equally complimentary: "Howes' circus will bear a very favorable comparison with the best that has ever traveled. It is under the most excellent management, the people connected with it are good people in both an artistic and a personal sense, the exhibition has more variety in it than is generally found, and there is nothing emblazoned on the bills that has not its counterpart under the canvas."[36]

After the St. Louis opening the show went into Illinois, Iowa, Minnesota, Wisconsin, and Michigan. It then worked its way to Texas and remained there until the end of November. A tour of the southern states followed, ending in Augusta, Georgia, in mid-January.

Unfortunately, Kelly's ownership of Howes' Great London was doomed to failure. Although it toured under his banner for four years, the show never achieved the financial success it deserved. The aura of bad luck persisted as the Great London suffered a fate similar to other shows at this time. The New York *Mercury* reported that of the twenty-four circuses catalogued by them in the spring only sixteen completed the season; the rest closed early or were felled by the sheriff's gavel.[37] Kelly's show was heavily indebted to the printing firm of James Reilly for unpaid advertising paper and Kelly was unable to make good. He had lost heavily in the aftermath of the Panic and more when the cashier of his Brewster bank embezzled funds and ran off to Africa to fight the Zulus. Early in 1877 James E. Kelly filed for bankruptcy at Whitehall, New York, reporting his liabilities at $216,000.

&

Howes' Great London, advertised to exhibit at Augusta, Georgia, on January 16, 1877, did not arrive until 1:00 p.m., due to some detention by the Port Royal Railroad, much to the disappointment of the crowd that had lined the streets awaiting the "Grand Mardi Gras" parade and to those who had planned on attending the afternoon performance. But at night, despite the inclement weather, a goodly gathering of Augustans, among whom was a representative of the *Chronicle and Sentinel*, witnessed a noteworthy performance. The leaping of Batcheller and Worland astonished the on-lookers. Mme. Dockrill well merited her title of champion female rider of the world. The performing elephants went through their exercises, appearing "as docile and sagacious as so many trained dogs." And William Conrad's trained dogs caused an infinite amount of amusement.

The man from the press expressed his full appreciation in stating:

It was by far the best circus performance ever given in this city. The performers are all first class, and are in large numbers. All the costumes are brilliant and new; the stock is all in fine condition, and the performance gave the most unbounded satisfaction to all.[38]

This was to be the final performance under the management of Kelly & Co., for that very night Sheriff Sibley closed the circus down and Constable Conner took charge of the money still in the ticket office. They were responding to a writ of attachment issued by the United States Rolling Stock Company for rent owed on their railway cars, the amount of the claim said to be $9,777.[39] Before the serving of the attachment, however, foreclosures had been issued by Richard H. Dockrill and James Reilly, who both held mortgage claims on the show—Dockrill for $18,200 and Reilly for $31,000.[40]

Howes' Great London was sold at auction on January 29, 1877, at Augusta, Georgia. An injunction to stop the sale was arranged through the office of the Hon. Samuel Blatchford, judge of the Southern District Court of New York; but it was ignored by local authorities because, it was determined, it had no validity outside the state of New York. So the sale proceeded as planned.

Some time after 10:00 a.m. the circus wagons full of equipment left the storage barns on Broad Street and wended their way—now more like a funeral procession than a parade—to the Lower Market where the sale was to take place and where a large crowd had gathered, anxious to witness the dismantling of a great circus.

Sheriff Charles H. Sibley explained to the gathering that everyone was privileged to buy and that the items would be knocked down to the highest bidder. But the sales were conducted by the sheriff in a way that allowed a buyer's bid on a single item to apply to large lots of the same, thereby circumventing the bids of those who were interested in only acquiring the original one. The only bidders revealed by the Augusta *Chronicle and Sentinel*, aside from the circus management, were a Mr. Craven, Mr. Tell, Mr. F. A. Jones, Mr. E. H. Gallagher, Mr. S. F. Ratcliffe, Mr. Lampkin, and Mr. Kalb and Mr. Miller representing the St. Louis Zoological Gardens. Only two were effective in achieving a high bid, Jones and Ratcliffe, each buying one horse.

The animals were the first to go. Each cage in turn was wheeled before the auctioneer. The high bids went to John J. Parks. Then came the chariots, seats, tents, poles, etc. They all went to John J. Parks. The sale was then moved to the Georgia Railroad yard where two tableau cars were sold, one for $1,000 and the other for $2,500. They both went to John J. Parks. The gathering returned to the Lower Market for the sale of a miscellany of circus equipment—wagons, poles, tents, blankets, mattresses, advertising, chandeliers, etc., etc., all going to John J. Parks. The horses and harnesses were put up next. John J. Parks was high bidder on all but two horses. The total sale realized $52,680.50.[41] Had the sheriff been up for bids as well? A skeptic would declare the "fix was on."

A few days later a serious effort was made to place the matter into a bankruptcy court. Frederick H. Miller, solicitor for the Metropolitan National Bank of New York applied to Judge Gibson of Superior Court of the Augusta Circuit for an injunction restraining all the principals involved—Sheriff Sibley, Parks, Reilly, Dockrill, Barnum, and Kelly—from moving the circus property out of Georgia and restricting them from consummating the sale; furthermore, enjoining the sheriff from paying to anyone the proceeds of the sale until after the resolution from the court. The logic for this was that the sale was scheduled before his solicitors were aware of the date and had no time to prevent it. The bill also stated that the bank "charges that the entire transaction is an arrangement, or using a current expression at the sale, 'a put up job,' to benefit certain alleged creditors of 'Barnum & Co.,' to the exclusion of others...."[42]

Why, we question, was "Barnum & Co." used in the legal documents to signify the circus company? James E. Kelly was the majority owner we believe, the show being sometimes referred to as Kelly & Co. Our guess is that, because of Kelly's indebtedness in areas outside his circus responsibilities, the identification of ownership was transferred to Barnum. We have, however, nothing to confirm this.

In response to the attempt at a retraining order, Richard H. Dockrill and James Reilly both issued documents to show cause why the bill of complaint of the Metropolitan Bank of New York should not be granted. Their defense was that because James Reilly, who held the mortgage, was about to foreclose on the circus property, Henry Barnum, as one of the proprietors, desired first to raise funds to pay off the employees to the sum of $16,000. Dockrill agreed to advance the money through a second mortgage. An additional $2,200 was given to pay off an indebtedness to the United States Rolling Stock Company with the understanding that the mortgage then be immediately satisfied.[43]

After all the lawyers were put to bed, Howes' Great London opened the 1877 season at Augusta on April 9 and 10 under the new management of John J. Parks, R. H. Dockrill, and Homer Davis. The reader may recall that Parks and Davis were former owners of the privileges on the show. We speculate that the patient Mr. Reilly was induced to hold off on his foreclosure and to continue as a silent partner.

The *Chronicle and Sentinel's* report of the season's opener was favorable, as one might expect:

> The show was previously the best we had ever seen, but since its re-organization, it is vastly improved by the addition of several important features. Entirely free from anything that could offend the most fastidious, it is an exceedingly entertaining exhibition. The visitor gets more for his money than he would in any other exhibition of a like nature, and all that is presented is certainly first class.[44]

The writer was most impressed with this year's featured performers. Mme. Dockrill, of course, headed the list. She "stands erect upon the bare back of her steed as confident and as much at home as if she were on *terra firma*. Her four-horse act is a marvel of equestrianism." He found the riding of Frank Melville to be superb as well. "Now dancing along the ground, now on the back of his beautiful steed, as he astonishes and delights the audience with the quickness and grace of his movements." The Victorelli Brothers, in his view, surpassed even the renowned Hanlon Brothers in their similar act. "Powerful and muscular, active and agile, they are specimens of manly beauty and strength." Fred O'Brien's leaping was awesome. His "double front somersault over the backs of five elephants placed side by side certainly entitles him to the belt as the champion vaulter of America, if not the world."[45]

In the afternoon of opening day a Mr. Barton made his first public entrance into a den of four tigers, after working with them for only two weeks. He had made himself famous with the locals by an earlier exploit, when a tiger escaped its cage at the winter quarters on Broad Street. With a number of spectators present, women and children among them, he grasped the cat's tail and kept it occupied until it could be re-incarcerated.[46]

Mme. Dockrill received her usual share of plaudits throughout the season. The Albany *Express* found her to be

Johnny Patterson

worthy of her title as Empress of the Arena, "for she certainly did the most reckless, daring riding that was ever done by a woman ... and it is safe to say that she has no equal among female equestrians, and that there are very few who can excel her."[47]

Irish clown Johnny Patterson joined during the season. He came to this country quite unheralded but quickly became a public favorite. "This man is very funny, as might be expected, his Irish dialect being natural and easy, and his jokes and stories told with a freshness somewhat at variance with the old, hackneyed style of years past," reported the Boston *Herald*. "He does not believe it necessary to characterize his people—the Irish—as a snobbishly-dressed, vulgar nationality in order to secure a laugh. Always refined and gentle as a woman, he is anyone's beau ideal of a genuine, highly-gifted Irishman," was an observation from Toronto's *Daily Leader*.[48]

The show, moving on a single section of cars, worked its way to Richmond and Washington, D.C., then into the New England states and Canada. It was back in the United States by early September, following a route through Ohio, Pennsylvania, West Virginia, Kentucky, etc., and closed at Pine Bluff, Arkansas, on November 29 before moving the outfit to Philadelphia for wintering.

In mid-August James E. Kelly's voluntary bankruptcy was announced in the New York *Clipper*. Among the principal creditors were P. T. Barnum for an unsettled menagerie account of $8,000; Nelson Robinson, $11,100; Mrs. Laura E. Reynolds, for services, $6,000; the Bulls Head Bank, $19,000; The Metropolitan Bank of New York, $47,100; Jules Nelson, of England, $80,000; and an unknown amount to Henry Barnum. As was indicated earlier, Kelly's total indebtedness was $216,000.[49]

The management went all out for the 1878 season, a sort of do-or-die gesture perhaps. They startled their competitors by assembling one of the finest company of performers in the country. Four of the greatest equestrians of any age were featured—James Robinson, considered by many as the champion bareback rider of the world; Mme. Elise Dockrill, the "Empress of the Arena" and daring four-horse rider; William Gorman, the "Wizard Horseman and Hurricane Hurdle and Jockey Rider"; and his wife Pauline Lee, elegant principal act and juggler on horseback. Captain and Mrs. Crapo were a unique exhibit to the show. They had recently crossed the Atlantic in their little boat *New Bedford*, which was also on view. The engaging couple related the story of this rough experience. An additional treat was the water queen, Vivienne Lubin, who performed acts of eating, drinking, and sewing while under water. [50]

The parade was still the leading feature of the show. The processional order as described by the Topeka *Commonwealth* was headed by beautifully caparisoned guards, then came the London Tally Ho Coach with a cornet band, richly attired ladies and gentlemen on horse, golden chariots, another band, five performing elephants, camels, and an array of Mardi Gras characters.[51]

After leaving Gilmore's Garden, the show went to Connecticut, Massachusetts, New York state, Pennsylvania, Ohio, Indiana, Illinois, Missouri, Kansas, Iowa, Wisconsin, Michigan, and on south, ending at Augusta, Georgia.

As before, it was well received all along the route. Below are favorable comments from Kansas. The Junction City *Union*:

> The street parade was perfectly gorgeous, the menagerie was good and the ring performance was decidedly the best ever given in Junction City. The London is truly an immense show, and in all respects, it is the best that travels.[52]

The Salina *County Journal*:

> We believe there was more satisfaction given by this company than any heretofore visiting our city.[53]

The Emporia *News*:

> It was a very fine procession, and by all accounts the animal show was quite satisfactory and the circus the best for years. The London show is the best that is traveling in the West, we think.[54]

Unfortunately, demon time was running out for the Howes' Great London. Serious losses to the performers and band members occurred with the burning of a baggage car at Moberly, Missouri, during a jump from Booneville to Hannibal on the morning of July 20. The car was carrying the private trunks of members of the company and some seventeen barrels of naphtha used for illuminating the tents. One of the containers was leaking the gas which, it is believed, was ignited by a spark from a watchman's lamp. The fire was discovered while the train was on a side track waiting for another to pass, but fear of an explosion deterred the saving of any of the car's contents. The loss was estimated to be $12,000 in clothing, money, and jewelry.

Another accident befell the company in Madison, Wisconsin, on August 27. A heavy storm hit around 6:00 p.m., blowing down the tent and injuring several canvasmen. The damage amounted to around $1,000 and, more costly, the night performance had to be cancelled.

The overhead was just too much for even the best of returns. High salaried performers ate heavily into the gross receipts. The advertising, as well, was far too costly. W. W. Durand, one of the most distinguished agents in the business was ahead of the show. In 1872 he had spent lavishly on advertising while leading the Great Eastern to astonishing success. Apparently he was continuing the practice with the Great London. For example, in Junction City a mammoth billboard was constructed to hold the show's paper, extending 200 feet on Washington Street and 100 feet on Sixth.[55] The show ended the season owing printer James Reilly some $60,000.

The fate of Howes' Great London was predetermined on November 4 in Philadelphia. At that time the partnership was dissolved when Homer Davis conveyed his interest in the circus to Parks and Dockrill. It would only be a matter of weeks before Cooper & Bailey would purchased the show from lien holder, Reilly.

III
THE BARNUM SHOW—
AFTER COUP

T HE 1874 CIRCUS UNDER P. T. Barnum's name went out under new management because the regular Barnum team was occupied with another venture. Although we have no intention of fully particularizing this change of direction—our main interest here being with the circus—a brief description might prove beneficial.

The Barnum organization took a bold turn this year by launching P. T. Barnum's New Roman Hippodrome, which was not a circus. There were no center rings as we know them. There were no clowns and but a few of the variety performances recognizable as circus acts. Instead, there was a large hippodrome track for racing horses, camels, elephants, and most anything else with legs. And with the track and the infield created by its oval, there was space for huge spectacle displays.

In his autobiography, Barnum referred to a "long-cherished plan of exhibiting a Roman Hippodrome, Zoological Institute, Aquaria, and Museum of unsurpassing extent and magnificence." His propensity for topping his previous achievements, strengthened by the financial success of the 1873 circus tenting season, supported the acceptance of such a scheme. It may even be that the creation of the hippodrome track for the 1872 and 1873 circus seasons had furnished the seed idea for such an undertaking.

Plans for his last "crowning effort" were set in motion in the fall of 1873. Barnum left for Europe in September and while there visited all the zoological gardens, circuses, and public exhibitions wherever he went, acquiring various novelties and valuable ideas. He then moved on to England where on January 2 he contracted with John and George Sanger to purchase duplicates of the entire wardrobe and paraphernalia connected with the "Congress of Monarchs," an impressive spectacle that had been exhibited at Agricultural Hall, London, some years earlier.

Meanwhile, Coup and Hurd leased the New York and Harlem Railroad Company property in New York City at Fourth Avenue and 26th Street that had been left vacant in 1871 by the opening of Grand Central Station at 42nd Street, and set about constructing a suitable venue. When the place opened to the public on April 27, 1874, the list of officialdom included P. T. Barnum, proprietor; W. C. Coup, general manager; S. H. Hurd, superintendent and treasurer; and Dan Castello, director of amusements.

The venture got off to a successful start. Newspaper ads claimed an average daily attendance of 20,000, with thousands unable to gain admission for the evening performances. This may have been an overstatement; but the place, which on completion seated somewhere between 10,000 and 12,000 spectators, was reported to have been filled almost nightly until the season closed on August 1.

The Connecticut Legislature issued a charter for the P. T. Barnum Universal Exposition Company, with a capital of a million dollars, on July 24, 1874. Barnum was recorded as president; W. C. Coup, as manager. Under the aegis of this enterprise, the immense Roman Hippodrome, with its aggregate of some four to five hundred men, women, and children, four hundred horses, and an assortment of camels, elephants and other quadrupeds, went on tour to introduce its unparalleled marvels to audiences outside of New York City, namely Boston, Philadelphia, Baltimore, Pittsburgh, and Cincinnati.

An advance crew of carpenters and other specialists preceded the show by several days in order to level the ground, prepare the hippodrome track and construct a tiered amphitheatre around it. The reader may recall that the practice of erecting a wooden structure for seating at each stand in advance of arrival had been instigated by Barnum's circus managers to some degree the previous years.

Following the Hippodrome's final performance on October 24, the weather being too cold to continue on to St. Louis and Chicago, the outfit was shipped back to New York City. All in all, the season had offered the most luxurious show of pageantry ever attempted on this continent. The various races, by both man and animal, contributed to a continuous excitement throughout the entirety of the matinee and evening programs. The claim of performing to 20,000 people a day was not disturbingly far from the truth. Barnum's "crowning effort," at least for this year, had been a crowning success.

Embarking on the Hippodrome project meant leaving idle a successful circus with accompanying equipment too new and too valuable to sacrifice at auction prices. The solution was to lease the title and equipment to another showman, along with the Barnum curiosities and many of the employees.

The new manager of P. T. Barnum's Great Traveling Museum, Menagerie and World's Fair for the seasons of 1974 and 1875 was John V. "Pogey" O'Brien. The choice of O'Brien to carry on the three year old Barnum circus name has raised more than a few eyebrows over the years. Skeptics have asked why a man of Barnum's stature would select a partner of such questionable integrity, a man whose legacy

John V. "Pogey" O'Brien

is the image of a scoundrel, who throughout a lengthy career in management developed a notoriety for dishonesty, coarseness, and a tolerance for grifters, qualities consistently purported by circus people and circus historians. And we have accepted them as representing the true nature of Pogey O'Brien. For example, C. G. Sturtevant wrote:

> ... he took mean advantage of his people, in small ways to mulct them of money they had due. He was also notorious in beating everyone he possibly could with whom he came in contact. His shows were a paradise for grifters, not in the ordinary sense of the word, for at the time many others carried grift with some discrimination, but on the O'Brien shows it was wide open. Gamblers, thieves and all manner of thugs were carried, and had protection both by fixers and a celebrated gang of canvasmen known as the "Irish Brigade," which were recruited with regard for their ability and love for a fight. This gang of iron fisted bruisers never lost a decision in the numerous clems the show got into with an outraged public.[1]

D. W. Watt, treasurer for the Forepaugh circus in the 1880s, accused O'Brien of knowing "little about the Ten Commandments." Chindahl, in his book, *The History of the Circus in America,* stated:

> If John V. Pogey O'Brien deserves mention in a history of the American circus, it is because he was a notable example of the dishonesty toward both employees and the public which characterized many shows. Gamblers and thieves became integral parts of his activities.[2]

Unfortunately, all of the above, although consistent in their charges, list no sources.

There is no doubt that grift was prevalent in the circus business at this time. Press agent Tody Hamilton has written that it was so common among showmen that certain "hangers-on" were said to own the "clothesline privilege" (the right to rob clotheslines on show day). "It is a well known fact that all sorts of games of 'chance' were conducted on the show grounds—in which the sucker had no

chance of winning whatever—from the shell games to rou-
lette. They were all 'skin' or 'brace' games."[3] By buying
privileges, grifters traveled along with the show; the proprietors of which received a "rake-off" from the proceeds of
their dishonest labors, and they often received protection
from the local police. "It was no uncommon thing in those
days for a town marshal or chief of police in small cities to
bargain with the show for immunity for everything done that
day and night, and to receive good money for this privilege
of robbing his neighbors."[4]

Thieves entered homes while the residents were at
the performance. During a Great London circus stand at
Janesville, Wisconsin, the house of David Cross was ran-
sacked and about one-hundred dollars taken. The same day
five dollars and some silver spoons disappeared from Dea-
con Lobar's home. That night J. C. Echlen had his horse and
harness stolen and Josiah Wright lost his buggy. But two of
the rapscallions met more than their match at Alderman Brit-
ton's house. They were surprised by the Alderman's wife
who gave them a merry chase until they barely escaped by
vaulting over a gate. The paper reported that several women
had their purses snatched and their pockets picked. "The
number of pimps, blacklegs, and diabolical scoundrels present from other cities was simply enormous," it read.[5]

Marketable privileges included the cook tent, candy
and lemonade stands, the program, the sideshow, the concert,
inside reserved seat tickets, outside admission tickets, as well
as various forms of grift. Outside privileges on tickets sold
for as much as $10,000 for the season. The buyer would hire
a number of men to travel with the show as salesmen. They
worked both in town and on the lot independent of the ticket
wagon and disposed of the tickets for whatever they could
get above the regular price and the percentage take by the
circus proprietors. In other words, every 50¢ ticket would

have to be sold for more than 60¢ for the grift to make a profit. "It was the policy of the show publicly to disown and excoriate these agents," Hamilton wrote, "while really it was responsible for and actually protected them."[6]

There were frequent reports of hawkers, gamblers, and thieves appearing out of seemingly nowhere. Supposedly, these were not circus people, but leaches who followed the show into town. An item in the Kenosha *Telegraph* revealed that on circus day there was a seller of cheap jewelry, and one dispensing "cement and solder." Two men from Waukegan—Buell and Rurtiss—tacked up a wheel of fortune on a pole near the post office and gambling took place unabated, protected by a license issued from the town's mayor's office. This "ten cent swindling operation" continued throughout the day and evening hours.[7]

But what of O'Brien? What was he guilty of? History has left us with little personal knowledge of him. We know he was born on January 29, 1836, the son of an Irish stone mason and resident of Frankford, Pennsylvania, at that time a suburb of Philadelphia. Beyond that, only two accounts by contemporaries supply us with most of what else we know, both written by former employees, one being submitted to the New York *Clipper* in 1872 by Birkit Clarke, who was O'Brien's treasurer the previous year.[8] Historian Stuart Thayer speculates that some of what Clarke wrote was designed to ingratiate him with O'Brien as a means of future employment. I leave that to the reader to determine.

Clarke tells us that O'Brien's education was acquired more from physical combat with his school mates than from an open text book. From such lack of devotion to learning, father O'Brien concluded that his son was more fit for labor than scholarship, so he put him to work mixing plaster. The job lasted until one day a larger boy threw an apple core at him, which ignited a bit of serious fisticuffs with our John

coming off the winner, only to receive a painful and dis-
heartening thrashing from his father. This may have been
the catalyst that caused his running away from home.

The mature O'Brien, Clarke recalls, was a man free
with everybody—"a king or a canvasman would be all the
same to him." He was always in good humor and his fund of
anecdotes was endless. He was an enthusiastic "kidder," and
then, after committing some such trickery, would explode
with laughter.

The other contemporary from whom we learn about
O'Brien is George Conklin, who left us with the best picture
of him in his book *The Ways of the Circus.*[9] Conklin joined
on with O'Brien in 1867 and was with him for several years,
eventually becoming the show's animal man. He obviously
knew Pogey better than most of his contemporaries. In *The
Ways of the Circus* he described the man as "rough and illit-
erate, yet with a large stock of native shrewdness." He remembered him as being fat and good natured, but a rough
and tough character, unable to read or write, but, as he
termed it, "hell on figures." The man suffered from asthma
which revealed itself in his wheezing voice and peculiar
laugh and required his sleeping in a chair instead of a bed.
He touched neither tobacco nor hard liquor. He found pleasure in attracting attention through his opulent attire, usually
appearing in a frock coat, pants made of blue broadcloth, and
a velvet vest. For hiring performers he changed to a double-
breasted vest with two rows of buttons inlaid with diamonds,
from which hung a large watch chain with each gold link set
in the precious stones as well. He was also very close with
money. Press agent Charles H. Day recalled that whenever
O'Brien stayed in New York City, he slept on a sofa in the
lobby of the St. Charles Hotel to save a dollar.[10] This miserly quality was both an attribute and a weakness.

O'Brien's ring barn, Darrah Street, Frankford, Pennsylvania.

At barely seventeen O'Brien became a stage driver in Philadelphia which lasted for a half-dozen years, during which time, through a life of frugality, he bought horses on the side. He then moved to Washington, D.C., where he drove a stage between that city and Alexandria, Virginia, and ultimately became owner or part-owner in the line. He entered the circus business in 1861 by renting horses to Gardner & Hemmings and going along as boss hostler. The next year he owned one-third interest in the show and retained it until he sold it to James E. Cooper a few weeks into the 1863 season. He then organized his own show that year, "Bryan's (sometimes referred to as Brian's) National Circus with Mrs. Dan Rice," for touring in Pennsylvania and New York state. Clarke writes that "from all I have heard regarding the concern, it must have been a very 'light waisted' affair." But, let it be noted, the show made money.

In 1864 O'Brien took out the Tom King Excelsior Circus with the leaper Tom King as the star. This was a partnership between O'Brien and Adam Forepaugh, with King being Forepaugh's man on the lot. It came about because Forepaugh had earlier supplied show horses, but when the payment came due he was forced to accept a share of the circus as settlement. After a route through Pennsylvania, Ohio, and Michigan, King left the show in Port Huron on August 20 because of a disagreement. On September 3 a card appeared in the advertisement columns of the *Clipper:*

> Having withdrawn from the associate management of O'Brien & King's Excelsior Circus, I take this method of requesting Mr. O'Brien to remove my name from the top of the bills.... I will give him twenty days from this date to do this. There are several honorable men in the Company, but I am sorry I ever associated myself with an omibus driver. Tom King.[11]

This appears to be the first negative imprint on the O'Brien reputation as a manager.

The O'Brien-Forepaugh partnership continued into 1865, when in April of that year the two men purchased the Jerry Mabie menagerie, consisting of twelve cages, two elephants and other animals. It was delivered at Twelfth and State Streets, Chicago, on the very day of the assassination of President Lincoln. This became the Dan Rice Menagerie.

Adam Forepaugh's early years were similar to Pogey O'Brien's. He was born in Philadelphia and began life there as a butcher boy at a salary of four dollars a month and board. He ran away from home when he was sixteen years of age and went to work for a Cincinnati butcher whose name was, quite coincidentally, John Butcher. He worked there for about a year and a half; after which he entered the butcher business in Philadelphia and continued in it until 1848, when he started running stage lines. During this time he also dealt in horses and cattle. A man of industry, in a single year during the war he bought and sold as many as ten thousand of them.

The managers eventually found they could not get along, so the partnership was dissolved after the 1865 season. According to Conklin, they divided the property by each man alternately selecting a wagon or an animal or some piece of equipment, a process that continued throughout the entire circus inventory. For the 1866 season O'Brien leased his animals to Yankee Robinson under George W. Sears' supervision, but there is no evidence that he took a circus on the road.

Forepaugh, on his own now, went out again under the Dan Rice title. From that year on, his circus enterprise underwent a gradual growth. When he started out with the Dan Rice outfit, the show had 110 horses, fourteen cages, a ticket wagon, and a daily expense of from $500 to $600. At the time the P. T. Barnum show was first organized, the New York *Clipper's* pre-season roster listed Forepaugh with carrying 140 people, 195 horses, twenty wagons and thirty-two cages. There were two elephants, six camels, a giraffe, a rhinoceros and the usual dens of exotic beasts. The two new canvases, housing the menagerie and the ring performance, measured 120 foot each. The sideshow, managed by Jacob Reed, was of little consequence. It included the Wild Australian Children, an armless man, feats of strength by William Sparks, and cages of monkeys and birds.

With the split from Forepaugh, Pogey O'Brien also increased his activity by acquiring more circus property. In 1867 he organized Whitby & Co., which included a menagerie, while again Yankee Robinson leased the so-called Mabie animals. In 1868 he owned both Bryan's Circus and Menagerie and DeMott & Ward's. In 1869 he operated Bryan's again, as well as Campbell's Circus and Menagerie, the latter managed by Hyatt Frost. These two shows were out again the following year with Campbell's under the management of James DeMott. His fifty cage menagerie that year was the largest in the country. Throughout this time he amassed so much property that in 1871 he put four outfits on the road, each with a menagerie—John O'Brien's, Sheldenberger's, Hardenberger & Co.'s, and J. E. Warner & Co.'s. In 1872 he had three shows—O'Brien's, J. E. Warner & Co.'s, and Kleckner & Co.'s.

He had a circus under his own name in 1873, which, perhaps in imitation of Barnum's "Great Traveling World's Fair," was called "John O'Brien's World's Fair on Wheels" (O'Brien's wife died suddenly at age thirty-seven just before the season began). The show exhibited under six round tops of canvas, five of which were described as "the worse for wear." The performing tent, however, was new. The menagerie was still the feature attraction, being made up of thirty-five cages. He also had interest in the Rice, Ryan & Spalding Circus that year. By now he was looked upon as a wealthy man and one of the most successful circus proprietors in the United States.

When he became associated with Barnum, O'Brien was young and experienced in the business, having been in management for ten years, longer than either Coup or Castello before they teamed with Barnum in 1871. In Clarke's 1872 article he was described as having a remarkable knowledge of show business. He possessed an elegant mansion in Frankford. Two blocks away his animal buildings covered an acre of ground and his nearby farm contained 500 head of stock. A perfect picture of an energetic and successful entrepreneur. And, with his large collection of animals, like Barnum, he was a man more interested in exhibition than performance. So, Pogey O'Brien in 1874, at age thirty-eight, would have been considered nothing less than an experienced and successful showman, capable of succeeding the team of Coup, Castello, and Hurd.

But if his reputation for dishonesty has merit, and one has to believe it does, what justified Barnum's association with him? Barnum, who was so sensitive about establishing his own image as a paragon of virtue and the circus under his name as a great moral institution, would never have accepted a partnership with someone of what we now consider an unseemly reputation. I can only conclude that it had not become a factor by 1874.

I refer to Clarke again. "Wherever he is known his word is equivalent to his note," Clarke attested in 1872, and "in excellent health, with ample wealth, and with an interesting family about him, he has all that can make a man happy in this world."[12] As late as 1880, George H. Batcheller and John B. Doris, who had been associated with O'Brien enterprises for eleven seasons, entered a card of appreciation in the New York *Clipper* which read in part: "In all transactions of whatever nature, we have always found you to be just and honorable, while large experience and sound judgment have been of incalculable benefit to us."[13] O'Brien's negative image, a result of cumulative improprieties, must have been formed after Barnum's selection of him as a partner.

Little has been made of the two years of O'Brien's tenure under the Barnum title. Arthur Saxon, the preeminent Barnum biographer, has given only slight mention to it; and Barnum, who was far more attentive to the fortunes of the Great Roman Hippodrome, was equally inconclusive in his autobiography. We know that, unlike the 1873 Barnum circus, this show moved on wagons but maintained the familiar elements of the prior circuses under the P. T. Barnum name. Three performances were given daily—10 a.m., 1 p.m. and 7 p.m. The Barnum autobiography was still on sale and still reduced to $1.50. The customary Barnum logo appeared on most of the advertising and Barnum's presence was felt even in his absence: "The happy face of Phineas Taylor Barnum has smiled so benignly upon *Observer* patrons during the past fortnight," the Utica paper read, "that all have anxiously awaited the advent of his traveling world."[14] And the bills spilled out the familiar Barnum line: "The Great Object Teacher of the Masses," "With Over 1,000 Assistants, Now Presenting 100,000 Life Lessons." Etc.

The museum and menagerie were still featured over the ring performance. There were fifty cages listed, which may have been a combination of both Barnum and O'Brien animals. Thirty-one museum wagons contained the exhibits of the previous years. The live curiosities included the familiar anatomies of Admiral Dot and the Fiji Cannibals, as well as the vocalizing head of the talking machine. The main tent, smaller than the previous year, seated some 5,000 spectators.

The two-ring format, originated by Coup in 1873, was continued in 1874. There were attempts by a few other circuses to incorporate the use of a second ring during the remainder of the 1870s, but none lasted more than one season. It is not known why the Barnum people stayed with it, particularly when their main interest was in launching the expensive Great Roman Hippodrome, and when the circus was being down-sized to a wagon show. Possibly they anticipated that other circuses would adopt a two-ring policy as a means of competing.

The show's level of ring artistry, under the equestrian management of James Cooke, the well-known English jester, was on a par with most of the major circuses. The male equestrian department was represented by the great Australian rider, James Melville, and sons George, Donald, and Frank. Holding her own alongside the Melvilles was Lucille Watson, who was judged by the Toronto *Globe* to be the finest equestrienne of her age.[15] They were supported by Arthur Nelson and his family of acrobats. The educated goat,

Alexis, was still a part of the Barnum family. And Herr Lip-
pard, who had recently arrived from Germany, showed his
mastery over some number of "brute actors"—a collection of
Phi Beta Kappa ponies, dogs and monkeys. James L. "Doctor" Thayer, the clown and ex-circus proprietor, represented
Barnum's interest with the show.

The so-called Fijis were still an attraction, but at this
time they appear to be counterfeit cannibals with the ability
to speak English in the manner of the American Negro. One
of their number had become quite pugnacious—representing
more the spirit of O'Brien than Barnum. So named Schiem,
but referred to as Jim, he exhibited a pugilistic propensity
when interpreting remarks by observers to be insulting.

"De white-ee man called me bad name, an I hit 'im,"
was his justification. On this particular occasion he was
hauled into court and fined twenty-five dollars.

Press agent Daniel B. Hopkins, showing lawyer-like
candor, related that the man was under a sentence of death in
his own country, that he had been elected congressman-at-
large by his island constituents but was impeached for sur-
reptitiously eating an English missionary's baby. One of the
attaches, however, being a bit more straightforward, admitted that the man was a "full blooded Negro" who had let the
deception out of the bag by speaking English.[16]

Privileges—the concert, candy, and sideshow—were
controlled by George H. Batcheller and John B. Doris.
These two men replaced the Bunnell brothers, who had
transferred their Annex to Barnum's Great Roman Hippodrome.

The show confined its 1874 tour to the Northeast.
After opening in Frankford, Pennsylvania, there were a
number of stands in New Jersey and, for a few weeks in mid-
July, in Canada; but most of the season was devoted to Pennsylvania and New York state. One might add that for both

the 1874 and 1875 seasons O'Brien did not exhibit in New York City or its environs as had the previous circuses under Barnum's name; rather, he stayed shy of the major cities as well as the areas in which the Roman Hippodrome was routed. He traveled the familiar path of his previous shows.

It was reported that on the occasion of the circus' opening night in Toronto some 2,000 people were turned away. And why not? Mr. Barnum was making one of his limited appearances of the season. "A good many people in Canada had heard of 'Old Barnum,'" asserted the *Globe* writer, "and they might be curious to know whether or not he had horns and hoofs."[17]

Adam Forepaugh's circus had now become a legitimate rival, being compared favorably to the Barnum organization. His 1874 eighth annual tour, the first year that the designation of "4-Paw" was used in the advertising, came out of winter quarters with an all new outfit—cages, harness, tents, seats, etc. The advertising boasted of two rings with an exhibition going on in each at the same time in an eight-center-pole tent.

The menagerie, the best feature, was housed under a canvas of six center poles. The courier for the year listed 60 different species, including everything from a rhinoceros to spotted and striped hyenas, from a black tiger to a wild hog, from a llama to a gnu. There was a pair of double-humped Bactrian camels and a giraffe. The ornithological department contained a pair of ostriches, a bird of paradise, a cassowary, and any number of other species. The three performing elephants were Romeo, Jr., Jenny Lind, and Young America. Forepaugh's menagerie was either the largest in the country or on the verge of becoming it. An impressed Baraboo *Republic* writer stated that in "Forepaugh's double hippodrome they will see more 'circus' than twenty ordinary traveling shows can exhibit."

The competitive breath of his organization was now being felt by the Barnum people. The rough tactics of his advertisers were disclosed to the public by a Wilmington paper: "Notwithstanding the threatening weather, the muddy condition of our streets, the murky atmosphere, and the malignant efforts of Adam Forepaugh and his agents to prejudice the public against the [Barnum] show, the performances throughout were well attended, and we have yet to hear the first person say aught against them."[18]

The Barnum 1875 season opened at Washington, DC, for a week beginning April 12, which turned out to be the only major stand. Most of the season was spent visiting the medium and smaller size cities in Pennsylvania and Ohio, with a few dates in New Jersey and Kentucky. Norristown, Pennsylvania, closed the tour on October 21 before the show went into winter quarters at Newark.

The season over, the Barnum/O'Brien relationship was terminated and the animals and equipment from both of Barnum's units were put up for auction. Unfortunately for O'Brien the Panic of 1873 lasted until 1878, and not only was business bad, he lost $9,400 in the collapse of the Jay Cooke bank. The lease ended on a sour note and Barnum was forced to sue for a $14,000 shortfall. To make matters worse, Adam Forepaugh took Barnum to court four years later seeking compensation for the value of the property sold as belonging to O'Brien—made up of horses, wagons, cages, etc.—claiming these items were really his.

Obviously, the Barnum name had not drawn as well as in previous years. A scribe for the Cleveland *Herald* explained it by stating: O'Brien "tried to make the public believe that he had a 'genuine Barnum', but it was like the equine quadruped which put on the lion's skin—the ears were too long."[19]

The second year of P. T. Barnum's Great Roman
Hippodrome also ended in failure. The attempt to operate
the show similar to a one-night stand circus was a mistake;
the large and cumbersome outfit was just too expensive.
With this the Coup and Barnum partnership came to an end.
It has been suggested that Coup's departure was provoked by
some animosity between the two. Coup never made a public
statement to confirm this; and if there was resentment it was
probably of minor concern. Still, there were contemporary
rumors. An item in an 1875 Cleveland *Herald* suggested
that Coup had seen impending trouble two years earlier and
"tried several times to slip out of the concern."[20] Such infer-
ences may have caused Barnum to make the following quali-
fication in his Advance Courier of 1876:

> In reply to many inquiries regarding my friend and late manager, Mr.
> W. C. Coup, I wish to say, that having labored hard and "made his
> pile," he preferred to retire, at least for a season. Meanwhile our
> friendship is uninterrupted. Mr. Coup is an efficient manager and a
> scrupulously honest and upright gentleman.[21]

The Barnum/O'Brien partnership had experienced
problems and a general lack of success in management from
the outset. For example, a sojourn into Canada during mid-
summer of 1874 was a financial disaster. In retrospect, the
Great Traveling World's Fair was merely the usual O'Brien
offering, barely held aloft by Barnum's name and famous
logo. And Barnum, who during his first three years in circus
management was so instrumental in exciting immense public
interest, was more involved in promoting his Roman Hippodrome than his circus. This was reflected by the local press,
who devoted great splashes of ink extolling the wonders of
the former and gave only superficial attention to the latter.

Conklin has written that O'Brien owed salary to
"Doc" Thayer at season's end, but when Thayer asked for his

money, he responded with, "Get it out of Barnum." This re-
fusal to pay up would prove costly. While the show was in
Canada in 1874 O'Brien had replaced his run down horses
with fresh stock. On his return to the United States he did
not report the exchange to the custom officers, but passed
through duty free. An angry Thayer threatened to report him
unless he made good on the unpaid salary.

"I don't care. Tell all yer want ter. I ain't scared,"
was O'Brien's reply.

So Thayer did just that. The result was a lawsuit initiated by the government against O'Brien over the unpaid
duties which dragged out for two or three years. In the end
O'Brien had to make good on the claim as well as a hefty
court fee.[22]

We can only surmise that O'Brien's years of good
fortune had peaked by 1874. In all probability, his financial
setbacks were serious enough to encourage desperate tactics
for acquiring the "almighty dollar." And, by all accounts, he
did. The sad portrait of Pogey O'Brien encompasses a fun-
loving Irishman who raised himself to wealth from nothing
through a natural shrewdness and toughness in business
dealings, only to revert to his primitive origins, ruthlessly
fighting over every apple core, and willing to profit from the
vulnerability of others; thereby leaving a legacy of dishonor.

&

The circus under Barnum's name was taken over by
the "Flatfoots" in 1876. The New York *Times* announced on
January 21 that Barnum had purchased the entire Great European Circus and Menagerie from Masseurs Smith, Nathans,
June and Bailey and was organizing "the most colossal show
ever collected." He "is about to produce the culminating
show combination of his lifetime, and will exhibit them in

the Centennial year to the greatest multitude of citizens and strangers that has ever upon any one great occasion or celebration been drawn together in the world's history." Smith, Nathans, June and Bailey, the paper continued, would enter his service as assistant managers.[23] Translated from "Barnumeze" this meant these men, the "Flatfoots," had combined their circus equipment and animals with remnants of Barnum's for another Barnum-type partnership and another of those "last crowning efforts." At this time Barnum was free from the distraction of his last "last crowning effort," the late Great Roman Hippodrome, and with but a single exhibition to occupy his creative thoughts. Consequently, we will detect a greater involvement in this circus venture than in the previous two years of the O'Brien management.

The use of the designation "Flatfoots" or "Flatfoot Party" arrived early in American circus history, but there is no certainty as to how it came about. According to C. G. Sturtevant, one source had it deriving from the flat foot of an elephant, elephants being important within their early exhibitions. Another, more acceptable, is credited to the insistence by these men that New York state was their territory for summer touring and the warning to their competition: "We put our foot down flat, and shall play New York state, so watch out."[24]

The original "Flatfoots" were John June, Lewis Titus, Sutton Angevine, and Gerard Crane. They were menagerie entrepreneurs who operated under the blanket of the Zoological Institute as early as 1820. When circuses began to travel, they crossed over into circus management as well. A shrewd and powerful bunch, they continually pressured other companies to buy stock and join them in an attempt to eliminate conflicting routes. They disbanded in 1837 following some financial reverses, but the firm was soon re-organized by another generation of men—James M. June, Gerald C.

Quick, Jesse Smith, and Thadeus and Jeremiah Crane. This group operated G. C. Quick & Co.'s and June & Co.'s Oriental circuses and invested money in many other arenic activities.

The use of "Flatfoots" in this volume, however, refers to Avery Smith, John J. Nathans, George F. Bailey, and, Lewis B. June, the last and perhaps the most successful of their line. Avery Smith was introduced to traveling amusements early on, as his father was a silent partner in the menagerie of June, Titus & Angevine. He began a career in circus management while still under thirty years of age and continued until the time of his death. Throughout those years he scrupulously avoided having his name appear in the advertising of any of the shows with which he was connected. He accumulated a large fortune from his labors, much of which was invested in New York real estate.

John J. Nathans began as an equestrian when he was around fourteen years old. Later, he became one of the first to ride four horses carrying a child above his head. He was connected with circuses as a performer, equestrian director, and manager from at least 1828 until leaving the Barnum organization. When he died he left an estate of close to half a million dollars.

George F. Bailey was the nephew of the old showman, Hachaliah Bailey, and son-in-law of early circus manager, Aaron Turner. When Turner died in 1854, Bailey took over the show and operated it successfully until he joined with Smith, Nathans, and June. Throughout his years of management he accumulated a fortune of over half a million dollars.

Lewis B. June descended from the famous June family of circus managers and "Flatfoot" proprietors. After entering the circus business in 1848, he spent most of his career as an advertiser.

George Fox Bailey

John J. Nathans

Lewis June

As a management combine, each of these men performed their specialty within the circus operation; Bailey saw to the day-to-day details of running a company, Nathans directed the performance end, June was concerned with the advance and advertising duties, and Smith served as treasurer.

The partnership was to be a 50-50 arrangement, with Barnum owning one half and Bailey, Smith, Nathans, and June the other, of which each was equal in stock and received no salary for their services. Barnum was to get a bonus of $10,000 above the profits for his name. He was to visit the show as often as was convenient after twelve visits appointed by his managers, but none were to require more than twenty-four hours journey from home.

These men were far different than Barnum's former partners. For one thing, they were nearly a generation older. In 1876 Smith and Nathans were both sixty-two years of age, only fours years younger than Barnum. Bailey was fifty-eight, and June was fifty-two. All were financially well off. And each had experienced a lengthy career as a professional dating back to the near beginnings of the traveling circus in America. They were show-wise, prudent, and not easily intimidated, something of which Barnum was certainly aware. It is quite probable that he desired the association of such veterans to relieve him of the anxieties of circus management and, having no son, for greater assurance that the Greatest Show on Earth would be perpetuated bearing his name.

The "Flatfoots" were associated with Barnum for five seasons, from 1876 through 1880. During their tenure they were steadfast in maintaining the standard that had been established by the original Barnum management. But unlike the Coup/Castello team, they were not innovative nor concerned with growth. They kept a steady, profitable course. Their most significant contribution was their ability to acquire strong performers, many of whom were imported from Europe.

Returning to 1875, the sale of the show property belonging to the P. T. Barnum Universal Exposition Company, formed when the Barnum organization took the Great Roman Hippodrome on the road, was commenced in the Hippodrome building on Friday, November 26. The apparent purpose was to sell off the stock and equipment of both the Barnum circus and the Roman Hippodrome. Attendance was quite small on this day, perhaps because of the unfavorable weather. The goods were sold by boxes, with the contents of each displayed on the seats within the Hippodrome building.

The "Flatfoots" were on hand and purchased a significant amount of wardrobe and animals. Barnum claimed they were acting for him: "My agents, Nathans, June & Bailey, bought in all valuable articles that I could use in building up my present great and only show, while nearly every showman in the country purchased duplicate animals and odd bits of my shows, for which I had no further use."[25] Although this was not a forced sale, the buying back of his own possessions through agents may have been necessary for Barnum because of the partnership arrangement of the Universal Exposition Company. Avery Smith purchased a box for $155 which contained a variety of dresses. A box of costumes, which sold for $180, an $85 box of band uniforms, and a large number of banners was taken by J. J. Nathans. The total sales this day came to less than $5,000.

The second stage of the auction was held in Bridgeport, Connecticut, on November 29 and 30. The "Flatfoots" took the lead in the bidding and came away with a sizable part of the live stock. On the first day, the draught horses sold for from $100 to $155 each with J. J. Nathans taking eighty-two of the one hundred on the block. Of the ponies, ranging in price from $70 to $180, and the two trick mules,

Pete and Barney, nearly all were bought by Nathans. He also purchased thirteen of the fifteen ring horses, which went for $200 to $400 each.[26]

On the 30th, wild animals and wagons were put up. Nathans' bidding bought him an ostrich for $200, a polar bear for $625, the elephants, Albert and Gipsy, for $3,000 and $3,150, six dromedaries for $200 each, a white muzzled sun bear for $75, a kangaroo for $55, a llama for $50, a sea lion for $400, thirteen performing monkeys for $220, and a riding goat for $50.[27] The "Flatfoots" were not interested in the wagons; they were planning to travel by rail.

We can get an idea of the size of the 1876 Barnum outfit from the recollections of Frank A. Robbins, who was with it that season. The performing tent was a 150 foot round-top with one fifty foot middle piece. There was a single ring surrounded by fifteen tiers of "blue" seats and thirteen tiers of "red" extras; but, he recalls, the "extras were in every day." The menagerie was a 100 foot round-top with three forty foot middle pieces; the museum tent, an eighty foot round-top with three forty foot middles.[28]

The 1876 roster for the "greatest show on earth" listed Barnum as manager and sole proprietor; John J. Nathans was general director; George F. Bailey, general superintendent; S. H. Hurd, financial director; and Thomas P. Jones, treasurer.[29] The advertisements touted four great circuses—P. T. Barnum's Hippodrome Heroes; Smith, Nathans & Co.'s Great European Circus; Lowande's Imperial Brazilian Circus; and the Company Carlos. The theme for the season was the American Centennial celebration.

In a letter to Samuel Clemens dated March 20, 1876, Barnum listed the patriotic elements to be used for this centennial year, undoubtedly the creation of his own fertile mind. At the start of the street procession, about 9 a.m., a number of cannons fired a thirteen gun salute. Within the

LET US REJOICE TOGETHER!
P. T. BARNUM'S
—AND THE—
PEOPLE'S DAILY GLORIOUS

Old-fashioned, Hail Columbia

Yankee Doodle, Centennial

4th OF JULY CELEBRATION
Inaugurated each morning about 9 o'clock by the brazen-throated
National Salute of 13 Guns when the
TRIUMPHAL PROCESSION
OF LIBERTY AND THE NATION,

procession was a large church bell which was apparently rung incessantly. It was the work of Meneely & Co. of Troy, New York, purportedly made from cannon captured in the late war. There was an abundance of American flags, a chariot mounted with a group of living characters in the costumes of the Revolution, a large platform car drawn by eight or ten horses carrying actors representing Generals Washington and Lafayette, each mounted on a white horse, with a live eagle perched aloft, and somewhere around was the familiar duo playing a fife and drum. Within the circus performance, the singing of national songs was introduced, lead by a chorus of several hundred voices. During "The Star Spangled Banner," cannons were fired as the Goddess of Liberty waved the Stars and Stripes, all concluding with the audience joining in the singing of "America," and "My Country 'Tis of Thee."[30]

The Centennial Tour season opened at the Rink on Third Avenue and 63rd Street, New York City, on April 27. Barnum was on hand and, as one might expect, had a short address prepared for the occasion:

> Ladies and Gentlemen: I presume it is because you know that I am a good judge of horses that I must necessarily be familiar with the ring. Well, the good people of Bridgeport don't think that I deal in "rings"—not political ones any way. But if an old showman can add any interest to the present entertainment by showing himself here tonight, I am well pleased to welcome you in person to witness the success of our enterprise. This show was not intended for permanent location in New York. The troupe will leave here in a few weeks, and go East as far as Maine, and West as far as Missouri. We expect a triumphant tour through the country.[31]

There was a strong company of performers, something that will prove characteristic of the "Flatfoot" regime. Martinho Lowande was featured. He was a member of the renowned Lowande family that appeared before the public for almost seven decades. His father, Alexander Lowande,

brought a circus to this hemisphere around 1867 with a roster
that included Martinho, his sister, Clarinda, and his brothers,
Natalio and Abelardo.   Now thirty-seven years of age—
dubbed "The Hurricane Horseman" by press agent Charles
Castle—Martinho was a four and seven-horse rider and did a
bareback carrying act with his seven year old son, Tony.

Starring honors were shared with Charles Fish, the
Champion bareback, somersault, and trick rider, and Jeanette
Watson, the principal equestrienne. There was also the Carlo
Family of riders, gymnasts and clowns consisted of brothers
George, William, and Frederick, who had operated the Carlo
Brothers' Circus for many years which toured Australia and
California.[32]

The menagerie was the usual assortment of exotic animals. It boasted of the only living hippopotamus in America, "a greater curiosity than 'Old Barnum' himself," and
said to have cost $25,000. There was a black rhinoceros, sea
lions, zebras, an eland, a gnu, giraffes, an Asiatic yak, etc.,
and by mid-season a fresh invoice of sea lions.

The museum was again under the supervision of W.
L. Jukes. A new feature was Capt. Georges Costentenus, a

Greek Albanian who was tattooed from head to foot. De-
signs included tigers, lions, snakes, and other animals. The
great publicist had a field day with this one. The ads read
that the tattooing occurred "in Chinese Tartary for engaging
in rebellion against the king."

> The prolonged and horrible agony of this combination of barbaric art
> and vengence necessitating over 7,000,000 blood producing punc-
> tures. I will give $50,000 for the production of half as extensive and
> perfect piece of tattooing, or for the correct deciphering of the hiero-
> glyphics upon his body.[33]

There was early skepticism from the public concerning the authenticity of the Costentenus tattoos, a suggestion
that Barnum was imposing another fake at their expense. To
allay this concern, a statement was included in the advance
courier which was attributed to Dr. Oliver Wendell Holmes
and other leading Boston physicians:

> This person is remarkable in combining in one exhibition a picture
> gallery, a menagerie of strange animals (in their portraiture), includ-
> ing one not unlike the dodo, and a proof of how much suffering man
> can inflict, or a man can bear, the constitution accommodating itself
> to conditions which might seem incompatible with health and even
> with life. It is the most perfect specimen of genuine tattooing which
> any of us have ever seen.[34]

The poor guy had to put up with a lot from the gawks
who paid to observe him up close. Some would pinch his
legs to see if the color came off. When this happened he
would frequently become angry and leave the platform; or,
in one instance in New Haven, "he gave the man a knock-
down blow."

The sideshow, or Annex, was again managed by the
Bunnell brothers. Its doors opened for business at 10 a.m.,
directly following the street procession, and again at 12 and
4 p.m., and preceding the evening performance. It included
"Yeppo," a creature purportedly captured during Stanley's

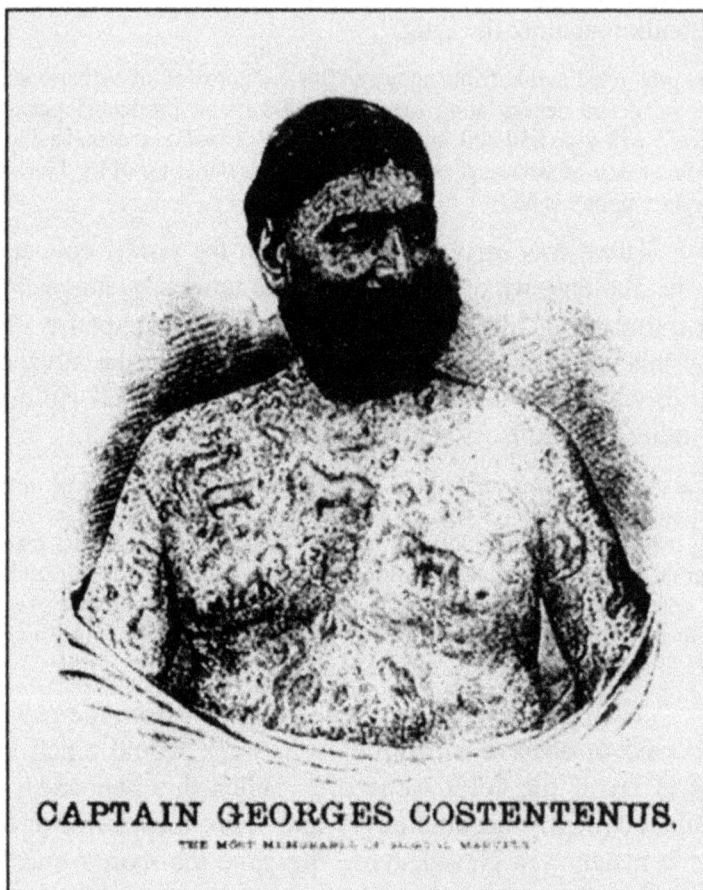

CAPTAIN GEORGES COSTENTENUS.

THE MOST REMARKABLE OF ROYAL MARTYRS

visit to Africa; Zoe Meleke, the Circassian lady; Mme. Ka-
thinka, German giantess; and Augusta, Johanna, and Her-
mann Reis, three German dwarfs.   There was a centennial
portrait gallery in which life-size automatons were animated
by a solid silver steam device designed by British inventor
Hiram S. Maxim.   Admission included a variety entertainment comprised of a full ballet and a minstrel troupe.[35]

The Barnum autobiography was still being sold in
conjunction with the show. The terms were the same—a
price of $1.50, "reduced from $3.50," 900 pages with thirty-
three full-page engravings, bound in muslin gilt, with a free
admission included in the purchase. This year a cheaper edi-
tion, with the same reading matter and illustrations, was offered for 50¢. After the tens of thousands of copies of the
autobiography peddled since 1871, apparently the book market had not dried; or, at least, P. T. was not ready to give up
on it.

Barnum claimed to have a hundred railroad cars,
most of which were made of steel to avoid smashing or tele-
scoping. The show owned all of them, including passenger
and sleeping cars.   Perhaps a more accurate account was
given by circus proprietor Frank A. Robbins, who was a
candy butcher on the Barnum show this year. He stated that
it moved on forty-five railroad cars, the stocks and flats being only thirty-two feet long and the sleepers forty and fifty,
and all of which would be equal to a twenty car show in our
century.[36]

The engagement at the Rink closed on May 6 after
only fair business. The road tour began two days later in
Hartford. After arriving in the middle of the night, the cars
were unloaded at the foot of Canton Street and the equipment and stock taken to the show lot at Colt's meadow.

The newspaper advertisements announced that Barnum would be on hand in person to address the audience.

Surprisingly the Hartford *Daily Courant* found both the morning procession and the arena performance less impressive than previous visits.

> Barnum's name is evidently depended upon, in connection with flaming posters and advertisements, to attract a crowd; for certainly the exhibition itself hasn't any merits such as people would be led to expect from the promises made, and its patrons yesterday were not as a rule satisfied, while very many were severe in their denumciation as the biggest humbug of Barnum's life.[37]

Through a letter to the editor within the same paper, a Mrs. A.C.C. expressed a strong opinion, calling the show the "Great Centennial Humbug Circus." The parade fell far short of advance advertising, she stated, and did not rate favorably with most second-class circuses visiting the city. But her greatest complaint concerned a general mix-up of seating. She had purchased her tickets in advance from the authorized agent at Z. P. King's Cigar Store, 270 Main Street, paying the extra price of reserved seats. To her astonishment, when she arrived at the circus grounds she was told by the uniformed men on the door that there were no reserved seats. In all probability, with more excursion people arriving than expected, the house had been over-sold; and, this being the first stand, the problem of handling crowds had not been adequately ironed out. Of course, this explanation would not have satisfied Mrs. A.C.C.

> Mr. P. T. Barnum pretends to love justice and fair play. This is the greatest humbug of his life! His speech expressing his regret that none of those who had any seats could see his wonderful "show" for the crowds who persisted in standing near the rope did sound very well in the afternoon, particularly as he promised that in the evening and succeeding performances everyone should have a seat and no one be allowed to stand and intercept the view; but when precisely the same words were repeated in the evening under precisely the same circumstances, they were greeted with the storm of hisses and other marks of contempt which they deserved.[38]

The following day a storm kept many people away, allowing those who did attend more comfortable accommodations. The weather was also the cause of some of the wagons to be loaded onto the rail cars early. The "greatest show on earth" was not off to the best of starts.

But there was quite a different reaction from the local *Telegraph* some months later when the circus was playing at St. John, New Brunswick, on July 27, 28, and 29. No seating foul ups marred this stand. "All Barnum's former efforts have been eclipsed by the colossal exhibition which he now presents to the public.... Every obstacle falls at his approach in his search for novelties, and the result is a show that is marvelous in the extreme." It went on to say that Barnum gave just what he advertised—never less, usually more—and people were not heard to complain that they did not receive their money's worth.[39]

Barnum was there on opening day and gave an address at both the afternoon and evening performances. Demonstrating a keen sense of his audience, he told them exactly what they wanted to hear—of his pleasure at meeting the people of St. John again, promising another visit in the future, how his show was greater than ever, what expense he had undergone to bring it to them, and that, his aim being to give them the best, he was confident they would leave the show grounds satisfied.[40] He might have even mentioned the sale of his new book, *Lion Jack*, described as a hair-raising romance.

The routing took the circus company into Connecticut, Massachusetts, Rhode Island, New Hampshire, Maine, New Brunswick, Nova Scotia, Vermont, New York State, Pennsylvania, Virginia, Maryland, and New Jersey, closing in Jersey City on October 5.

Avery Smith died in his home at Newark, New Jersey, on December 26. This led to a controversy between the

active managers and Barnum. Mr. Barnum wanted to buy
Smith's share of the partnership. Nathans, Bailey and June
felt that it would create an imbalance in the ownership, giving Barnum greater control, and that because they were doing all the work they deserved the financial return of a full
half of the profit. In a letter to Barnum, Bailey responded
with: "Our partnership was intended to be equal in stock and
we to receive no salary for our services. Mr. Smith services
did not amount to but little. He was good to consult & besides that was but very little. It was not his plans that organized the present show; therefore, I can't see that you are
the loser by his death and surely it would not be equal to
have you own more stock than us and we do all the work the
year around. Your name and percentage that you do get was
& should be for the whole of it."[41] Ultimately, Barnum con-
ceded to leave the previous arrangement as it stood through
the contracted period ending on March 1, 1880.

There was another disagreement at this time. Barnum was apparently trying to lease his name to Jim Myers'
circus in Europe and perhaps to other amusement organizations in this country, for in the same letter as the above Bailey has this to say:

> It is very hard work now to make the public believe that you have any
> interest in the show, only that we give a price for your name. Now
> when it is known that you sell your name to other parties for show
> [business] like unto ours all over the country, you can see what effect
> it must have on the public's believing that you have anything to do
> with the show. It's a daily talk now in Iowa that you have nothing to
> do with the company but only rent your name. Can we afford to put
> up capital and pay you bonus and allow you to rent your name to
> other show enterprises and do all the work?

He then goes on to spell out some of the terms of the contract:

We like you as a partner and we are willing to remain for 2 or three years partnership and upon these terms. 1ˢᵗ stock divided as it is. We will ask no compensation. Conduct the [business] the best that we know how to make and save money. You to receive ten thousand dollars more than half of the profits and if you insist upon selling your name in Europe you shall have that right, but not in any part of the northern hemisphere unless we have our share of the proceeds.... You to visit the show as often as it's convenient at your option after 12 times appointed by us. If your health will permit the contract, or partnership to run for 2 or 3 years the same, if you should die, for the interest of your heirs. This is a very just and equal arrangement for us to enter into for both sides. You can't find for any price men that will take hold and work for the interest of the show as we do, pay them what you will.

Although the Chicago *Inter-Ocean* reported that "not a few circuses have 'burst up' this season, and only the more rigorous and substantial organizations have been able to weather the hard times,"[42] the Barnum people ended up with a profit.

Barnum's first season of the "Flatfoot" regime was acceptable—the word Barnum used was "satisfactory"—but not spectacular, a far cry from his first under Coup and Castello. As we have indicated, the present partners were were conservative showmen who had many years of successful operation and were not about to alter their style. But times were changing. Following the early Barnum example, circuses grew larger and able to cover a greater area within a season.[43] The three major competitors had turned to rail travel, Howes' Great London in 1875, Cooper & Bailey and Adam Forepaugh, in 1876. The art of press agentry was immensely improved, and more money was being laid out for advertising. Talent, both foreign and native, was more varied and easily available, thereby equalizing performance quality from one show to the next. It was the occasional novelty act or specialty component, properly publicized, that could make a season.

In 1878, when asked about advertising costs, Barnum responded that it was a heavy drain but necessary to make a profit. He said that his pictorial printing for the year had cost $43,000 and that newspaper advertising was even higher.[44]

The circus' first stand in 1877 was at Gilmore's Garden, the former Hippodrome building, for four weeks beginning April 9 before starting the traveling season at Danbury, Connecticut, on May 7.[45] The company was made up of 317 employees, twenty-five cages of animals, thirteen museum cages, twenty-two baggage wagons, one ticket wagon, four tableaux cars, fifty railroad cars, 117 horses, seven ponies, four elephants, and four camels. The street procession succeeded in extracting the desired wonder from the crowds that lined each local thoroughfare to assess if indeed it lived up to the advertising.[46] One price of 50¢ admitted the ticket holder to all three venues, but the arrangement on the lot was such that placed the ring tent at a distance from the museum and menagerie in deference to patrons who preferred to set no foot further than the depository of exotic animals and artifacts, the ring performance being, to some, anathema. The Decatur, Illinois, *Daily Republican* assured their readers of this grouping, noting that anyone visiting them would not be aware that a circus was anywhere in the vicinity.

The well-traveled Charles Fish was the top rider this year. Apprenticed to James McFarland around 1856, he learned his art on the old Spalding & Rogers circus. His later engagements took him to Canada, South America and, most recently, to Europe, where he appeared before royalty. During his prime he earned the unofficial recognition as "Champion Bareback Rider of the World." As a performer at this time, he was quite in his prime at barely twenty-nine years old.

The introduction to this country of six Trakene stallions was the major novelty of the season, and would become a continuing audience favorite for the remainder of the "Flatfoot" management. They were advertised as belonging to the King of Prussia and stabled at Trakene, near Poland, kept there to be trained for staff officers. When they were bought by the circus at $5,000 for each of the six, the horses were wild and had never been shod, so it read. Actually, they were purchased by George Bailey on one of his trips to Europe from Jim Myers, proprietor of the American Circus in Paris.

All of the horses in Europe used for circus purposes were trained by only two men, Barnum announced, Carl Antony and his father.

> I secured the services of Carl Antony. He trained the horses, but no American horseman was able to do the feats with them that he did, and so I was rather obliged to give him a permanent situation in my show. I made a permanent engagement with him, as you know, and so he is with us now. More than this, his father is in my services also, and is receiving a large salary. With these two men, I have at my command the greatest horse-trainers in the world.[47]

The museum again featured Capt. Costentenus, the living gallery of tattooed dexterity, which motivated the Janesville *City Times* to suggest that he "clings to Barnum as the many colored illustrations do to the skin he exhibits." The ladies were a bit cautious of the fellow because of his nudity, a necessary condition for displaying his dermatological art work. But the *Times'* man assured us that the Greek was no humbug because, as he wrote, "we walked boldly up and pinched and jabbed pins in the fellow until we became satisfied that his hide was natural."[48]

Admiral Dot was back and, being fully dressed, drew admiring glances from the same set of females. A sample of unparalleled mechanical ingenuity, Gideon's Band, was

P.T.BARNUM'S $30,000 STUD OF TRAKENE STALLIONS COMING.

AS THEY ACTUALLY APPEAR
AT EACH PERFORMANCE.

represented by an automaton of twelve pieces, all life-size playing different instruments and capable of a variety of tunes.

Not to be confused with the museum, there was again the Bunnell brothers' Annex, so called to circumvent the unfavorable label of "sideshow." This place was not included in Barnum's 50¢ for all price of admission; but the public was assured that, once inside, the single ticket paid for at the entrance would admit the holder to all parts of the entertainment and that all exhibitions, concert included, would be given in this separate pavilion. The place opened directly following the parade and performed continuously from 10 a.m. to 10 p.m.[49]

The railroad war this year was a nuisance for traveling shows. The Barnum people encountered the problem in July during a move from Elgin, Illinois, to Laporte, Indiana. Normal travel was interrupted by disturbances when the Lake Shore road was unable to receive the Barnum trains from the Western road, which was to haul them from Elgin to Chicago, forcing the company to remain in Elgin over another day. Then at midnight the trains left there for Chicago with the understanding that the show must protect their own property and persons. The locomotives had upon them placards which read, "This train is under the protection of the United States Government." A U. S. Marshal accompanied it and all the company carried weapons. Asa Berry, the master of horse, had his force all armed with six-shooters; Charles McLean commanded the canvasmen, forty in number; and Ben Maginley had charge of the performers. The ladies and children were sent forward on a regular passenger train.[50]

The tour ended at Philadelphia on November 3. The menagerie animals were taken to the New York Central Park Zoo and the wagons and equipment to quarters in Jersey City for repair and storage. The mileage for the season totaled 8,299. Throughout the tour there was the usual number of camp followers—peddlers and "fakirs"—accompanying the show; from whom, no doubt, the veteran and wiley management abstracted a portion of profit.

We cannot complete our story of the 1877 season without relating the great tragedy that befell the show. The advertising car was lost on the morning of August 29 on Four Mile Creek, three miles west of Altoona, Iowa, and seven miles east of Des Moines. There had been heavy rains in that area and the creeks were all swollen to overflowing, in some places the water being up even with the railroad tracks. In traversing Four Mile Creek the train's speed carried it nearly across the overpass before it broke through, the pressure of the water having weakened the bridge supports, causing it to collapse and the train to go with it. The tender buckled up over the engine, killing the engineer and fireman; the baggage cars and advertising car, which were directly behind, rear-ended each other; the passenger cars were submerged into the river bed; only the Pullman remained on the track. Eighteen men died on the spot and others died later. Seven of Barnum's advance crew were killed and five others injured. The injured were taken to Cottage Hospital in Des Moines, the only one in the city at that time.[51]

When Barnum was informed of the care that had been given his men, he contacted the hospital officials and offered to give a lecture in Des Moines as a benefit. When about a month later he arrived in Des Moines, he went directly to the railway offices and thanked the men and women who had been instrumental in caring for the dead and injured. In the afternoon he attended the State Fair, which was (not coincidentally) in session, and addressed the crowd from the Administration Building. And in the evening, as promised, he gave a temperance lecture from the stage of Moore's Opera House to an overflow audience.[52]

Horses dominated the 1878 season. The Trakene stallions under the direction of Carl Antony were again the main attraction. The animals amazed audiences by their exhibition of equine sagacity and docility. "These animals are magnificent specimens of their genus, and their evident intelligence and appreciation of what is required of them is nothing short of astonishing."[53]

There was also a group of seven so-called Russian stallions exhibited, said to have been bred in the stables of the Czar and purchased for $42,000. Trained by Antony, they went through a series of military maneuvers and other evolutions—forming a line, rising on their hind feet to salute their trainer, moving their bodies in unison as the trainer rode in various directions, repeating the same with their forefeet upon platforms, and closing with a unison demonstration of galloping, changing their course, waltzing and halting on word command.

Add to this Mameluke and Pasha, Hungarian stallions performing an act called "The Dawn of Liberty," and Sankissoff, a beautiful gray horse, displaying a leaping ability by going over a high, canvas-covered frame painted to resemble a stone wall, and over the backs of other horses placed at equal distance around the arena.   There was also Mlle. Adele, "Queen of the Sidesaddle," and her stallion tandem team executing *acts de manège*.   Still more. Trick Italian stallions from the stables of King Emanuel I, so read the publicity—"As Obedient as Soldiers, as Playful as Kittens, as Cunning as Foxes, as Pretty as Pictures, as Affectionate as Lambs, as Funny as Monkeys."[54]

The menagerie featured a marine aquarium, a school of live sea lions, a black rhinoceros, and a number of elephants, along with the usual caged and tethered creatures. Barnum had purchased two elephants in Europe in the fall of 1877, which were to be brought over and with the eight he already had were to be trained to perform together.   In the 1878 *Barnum's Illustrated News* there is reference to "My Elephant Actors," that were schooled and exhibited by Felix

McDonald, which might lead one to believe they were indeed worked in the ring. I have found nothing else to justify this.

The museum was still headlined by Capt. Costentenus and his ink-frescoed anatomy—"Over Seven Million Blood-producing Pictures." This overshadowed the suit of jeweled armor supposedly worn by Joan of Arc, and the historic portrait gallery of oiled replicas of illustrious from the past. The live out-sized and under-sized were present; six foot seven inch Col. Goshen, the Palestine giant, was outranked by "the smallest living dwarf," Brig. Gen. Spec, advertised as twenty-five inches tall.

W. L. Jukes' mechanical marvels were still on exhibit, and still operated by a silver miniature steam engine. There was Gideon's Band, nine grotesquely attired automaton musicians, which played pieces, from operatic arrangements to military marches—"moving their limbs, eyes and all parts of the body like life." "The Aroused Lion," a frightening replica of the king of beasts, roared ferociously at the gawkers who passed his way. For true believers there was a perfect model of the Apostolic Clock in Strasbourg Cathedral; just as for the appreciation of teetotalers there was "The Temperance Home; the Curse of the Bottle," groups representing "the Blessings of Temperance and the Terrors of Drunkeness." And many more items were on display that moved by gears and springs, from boxing clowns to a sleeping beauty to Swiss Bell-ringers and even a manikin circus. No other show could compete with this. Mr. Barnum did not leave out anyone with 50¢ to spend.

A report by the *Clipper's* Hartford correspondent incited a controversy by suggesting that George F. Bailey publicly acknowledged the show as his own by refusing to honor passes issued by Barnum. He charged that Barnum, as a member of the Connecticut State Legislature, had presented each of his colleagues with complimentary tickets at the end of the last season and that Bailey refused to recognize them, even one held by the Governor.[55]

If one wondered how that would be received by the Barnum camp, he had only to wait for the *Clipper's* next issue. A letter to the publisher dated May 15, sent by Bailey, specifically designated as "Manager for P. T. Barnum," read: "I see in your issue of May 18 an article setting forth that I had refused, at Hartford, at the doors of the show, tickets that were given by Mr. Barnum to the Governor and the Legislature of Connecticut. Your correspondent does not tell the truth—there were no such tickets refused at that or any other place by our door keepers, or by myself."[56]

Directly following was a letter from Barnum dated May 17, displaying the usual Barnum dander when the ownership of a circus under his name has been questioned. He began by admitting a problem had existed. "Your agent and mine had a misunderstanding at Hartford. According to my view, my agent was in the wrong. I think a like error will not occur again." It was not explained what the misunderstanding was. "All that stuff about my manager refusing to recognize tickets given to the Governor of Connecticut is a fabrication, without one word of fact in it." Then came Barnum's explanation of his position as owner of the circus:

The pretense that I am not the owner of my show, as well as the slurs and innuendos which your correspondent makes, are false, unjust, and unworthy of your paper. It is a stale dodge of envious and unprincipaled showmen to pretend that I hire out my name; but the truth is that I own every dollar of my own and only "Greatest Show on Earth." I travel with it almost continually during the summer; I purchase and hire all the novelties; write my own show-bills and advertisements at the beginning of each season; and I exhibit scores and hundreds of rare and expensive wonders which I do not even advertise. My attractions are new and none of them ever belonged to any other exhibition in America. The money invested by me in my

unparallel show amounts to more than was ever before put into any
two or three traveling shows in any country, not counting the cost of
my own trains of railroad cars, which transport my people, animals
and paraphernalia through the country. I will cheerfully give your
Hartford correspondent, or any other man, *ten thousand dollars* if the
bare expenses of my show for the last seven years have not been more
(probably treble) than the entire gross receipts of any show that ever
traveled in America or Europe. If he will pay for the time required
from my bookkeeper, he shall have free access to all my account-
books for the above purpose.[57]

Let us try to sort through this Barnumeze for what
might be factual. He most likely invested his own money for
most or all of the current show property. He did secure the
novelties in the museum and most of the animals in the menagerie. To say that all of his attractions had never belonged
to any other exhibitor in this country is nonsense. He did
write much of the advertising copy in advance of the season.
He did not, as he suggested, travel with the company almost
continually, but only occasionally. And alas, one wishes the
man from Hartford had accepted the Barnum offer to look at
the account books, then we might have a clearer picture concerning his vaunted daily expenditures.

Barnum also enclosed a copy of a letter sent to him
by Governor Hubbard dated May 18 which read: "It is *not
true* that your pass was refused. Quite the contrary. Who
would dare refuse the pass of the great Emperor of Showmen?"

Be patient, reader. There is more. A letter dated May
26 from the no-name Hartford correspondent was published
"that equal opportunity should be given." We submit his ar-
gument forthwith:

Notwithstanding Governor Hubbard's published denial, that gentleman did present a pass to the doorkeeper of the Barnum show on the
afternoon of May 11, in the city, and *was refused admission on it*; after which he left the grounds, followed by Chief-of-police Chamber-

Chamberlain, who witnessed the whole transaction; and after a moment's conversation together they returned, and the Governor then passed into the show: *not on a pass however*, but as the chief executive officer of "The Land of Steady Habits," introduced as such by Mr. Chamberlain. On May 22 I called on both of these gentlemen. Mr. Chamberlain unhesitatingly pronounce my story correct. The Governor at first declared he was not refused admission; but when I had refreshed his memory with the facts, as above stated, and to which I was an eye-witness, *he acknowledged that he was refused*, and explained by saying the ticket he presented was not a pass to the Barnum show, but a pass to another and altogether different exhibition. From newspaper accounts published in the vicinity previous to the appearance of the show in Hartford, it seems that Bailey was refusing Barnum's tickets all along the route, and *The Hartford Sunday Globe* of May 12 published an article on the subject from their Meriden correspondent, which will prove interesting inasmuch as it calls for an explanation from Bailey for refusing Barnum's passes in that city. I present it in full: "Barnum's business manager, Bailey, refused checks signed by Mr. Barnum, and entitling the holder to seats in his Hippodrome or any other organization bearing his name. Some newspaper men would like an explanation, as they were given in lieu of local notices." Mr. Barnum wishes to make it appear that I manufactured and published this attack on him and the show that bears his name because his agent and myself had a misunderstanding. The fact is, *I had no misunderstanding with anyone connected with the show*. I did my business with Mr. Lawrence, the press-agent, and found him a courteous gentleman. I published facts as they appeared to me from personal observation, and I was not influenced by prejudice; and, furthermore, I did not attack Mr. Barnum in any way. What I said about Bailey & Co. owning the show I had good reason to believe was true.[58]

I leave it to you to be the judge and jury here and to decide who is the errant knave and who the winner of this duel of epistles. We might add that two weeks after the publication of this last letter there was an announcement that Barnum had decided to travel with the show during the entire season. He may have traveled with it for some dates in New

England and New York state, but it is certain he did not remain for the entire tour.

We know he was with it when the show exhibited in Geneva, New York, on July 5, however, for he addressed the audience from the arena, telling them it was his sixty-eighth birthday. Later he was serenaded at his hotel by band leader J. H. Withers and the group circus musicians. But on November 5 he was elected State Representative from Bridgeport. It would seem quite impossible to run for office while with a traveling circus.

&

We have come to the last two years of Mr. Barnum's career as a showman when his name stood alone in a circus title. From 1871 through the season of 1880 the name and personal logo of "P. T. Barnum" was heralded in large, engaging type on all of the thousands of promotional materials distributed by his many advertisers, creating a public presumption that he was the sole owner of "The Greatest Show on Earth." He often embellished the perception by calling his financial partners and on-the-lot managers his "agents" and by repeatedly revealing the huge expenditures he made for the various features of his circus. "I have freely and gladly invested more than a million dollars in the production of this Museum, Menagerie, and Arenic Miracle," he once boasted in a published letter to the citizens of Clinton, Iowa, and, "I will take pride in traveling with [the show] for most of the season."[59] He has repeated this embroidery on many other occasions.

An article in the St. Louis *Post-Dispatch* suggested the extent of Barnum's presence with the show for this year of 1879. It estimated that during the season he would travel some 15,000 miles, accompanied by his young wife and his secretary and valet and Mrs. Barnum's maid. As it was so written, following breakfast each morning, the entourage took a personal palace car to the place where the circus was exhibiting; then, upon arrival, a private coach conveyed them to the best hotel. But care was taken for Barnum to arrive at the lot in time to address the matinee audience from the arena. There is no way of knowing how many individual stands this mileage represents; but as it was reported, "in every town in Michigan he was complimented by local bands of music."[60] The information was obtained from an interview with Barnum, so, judging from past practice, the figures are apt to be bloated to support a public notion that he most always traveled with his circus. It is hard to imagine that at his age and health, he would devote that much time away from Bridgeport, not to mention that his estimated travel distance is more than double the 6,441 the route book lists as the total miles covered by the circus for the year.

Again referring to the route book, we can envision the size of the show for 1879. There were 316 people on salary. Fifty-one railway cars were used to transport everything. The rolling stock included twenty-three baggage wagons, twenty-seven animal cages, twelve museum cages, five tableau cars, and one ticket wagon. There were 135 horses and fourteen ponies. The ten elephant herd was the same size as the show's two major competitors.

The female riders, five in number, were the strength of the arena entertainment. Linda Jeal's riding and leaping through hoops was applauded by Chicago's *Inter-Ocean*: "She is a remarkable hurdle-rider, and the attractiveness of her performance is enhanced by the fact that she and her horse make a clean leap through a circle of fire." Emma Lake, in her *manège* act, "gives a beautiful exhibition of saddle-riding on her splendid trained horse, displaying horse-womanship to win the admiration of the spectators." Katie

Stokes was considered one of the best of bareback riders. "There is a grace and finish to her acts, and her balloon and banner leaps are good, honest jumps." Mme. Elise Dockrill, the Great London having gone to grief, was here; and her riding, particularly her four-horse act, still excited audiences (unintentionally so in Chicago when on August 12 her horse struck the wooden ring bank, causing her to be violently thrown to the ground). And finally, there was the pad riding of Lizzie Marcellus, the highly esteemed wife of W. H. Stowe.[61] These ladies deserved and earned good money for their work and Barnum was willing to pay top dollar to them. We learn that Linda Jeal's salary was $125 a day. "She is the most wonderful female rider in the world," Barnum acclaimed. "Her feats of throwing herself upon her horse's back with her hands holding the strap encircling the horse is marvelous." And Mme. Dockrill drew $900 a week, plus expenses for her six horses.[62]

The entire ring performance was of high caliber. The trained stallions, under the whip of Carl Antony, amazed audiences for the third year in a row. "These animals are magnificent specimens of their genus, and their evident intelligence and appreciation of what is required of them is nothing short of astonishing."[63] The three Herbert Brothers were meritorious in their gymnastic feats; as was Linda Jeal's husband, William O'Dale Stevens, in his acts of balancing. There was also the Langlois Brothers, an Egyptian juggling troupe; Signor Sebastian's carrying act with his son Louis; the leaping of John Batcheller; and the clowning of Charles Seeley, W. H. Stowe, John Robinson, and James Holloway.[64]

The traveling season opened for a week at the Capitoline Grounds in Brooklyn on April 28. The show then followed a route through Connecticut, Massachusetts, Rhode

Island, Maine, New Brunswick, Nova Scotia, Maine, New Hampshire, Vermont, New York state, and back into Canada. This was one of only a few circuses that went into Canada this year; a heavy duty on bringing circus equipment across the border amounted to over $6,000. From Canada the route led into Michigan, Illinois, Missouri, Indiana, Ohio, West Virginia, Pennsylvania, Washington, D.C., Maryland, Delaware, and New Jersey, closing at New Brunswick, October 18. The total receipts amounted to $429,765, from which Barnum received $36,572. This would probably place the total net income for the season in the $60,000 range.

A continuing annoyance to Barnum was the lingering law suit brought against him by Andrew Haight, George DeHaven, and Robert E. J. Miles, former proprietors of America's Racing Association. Their show was a competitor with Barnum's Great Roman Hippodrome for a brief time in 1875; and, to Barnum's disrelish, an imitation of it. The animosity and legal maneuvering go back to that rivalry.

In early April of 1875, Barnum accused certain impostors in Cincinnati of copying his bills, posters, cuts, and advertisements in an attempt to pass as the authentic Roman Hippodrome. Certainly the show was a mirror of the Barnum model—the tent was comparable and the program followed an almost identical format, with the opening spectacle bearing a title the same as Barnum's, *The Congress of Nations*. There can be no doubt that the Association was attempting to take advantage of the earlier success of the Great Roman Hippodrome.

From its outset, the Racing Association encountered nearly six weeks where there was scarcely a day that the tents were dry, and consequently the attendance and receipts were small. The establishment being an immense concern and the number of employees large, the expenses were heavy and a plenitude of obligations were incurred. Organized with the idea of usurping the prosperity of the Roman Hippodrome, the plan was to route the show a few weeks in advance of Barnum's as it worked toward New England where there were already at least five circuses traveling. It "sought to be the first over the northern route and 'scoop' everything else; but it was badly 'worsted,'" a Rochester paper observed.[65]   And, indeed, the show came to grief at Ogdensburg, New York, in mid-May, cutting the rivalry short, almost before it began.

In October of that year Barnum responded to a report that the America's Racing Association had commenced a suit in Cincinnati against him for injury to their business. He wrote to the *Clipper*:[66]

> Bridgeport, act. 2,1875.
> Frank Queen, Esq.—Dear Sir: I see by the newspapers that the so called American Racing Association and International Hippodrome have announced that they have sued me in Cincinnati for injuring their business. This is the first that I have heard of it. The fact that they telegraph it to Eastern papers proves that it simply for effect. This concern advertised attractions which they had not got, and nobody but I exhibited. My advertisers exposed them. Their manager then signed an agreement not to do so again, and he and my manager passed receipts in full. This is all there is to it, and it don't amount to shucks.
>
> P. T. Barnum

The Racing Association managers claimed that Barnum and his partner, W. C. Coup, had conspired to destroy their organization by hiring men to derail their train and injure their horses and, in general, to encumber their ability to arrive at scheduled dates; and that this danger necessitated the use of a pilot engine, sent out in advance of the show train to uncover evidence of sabotage. Such rascality, they claimed, had forced the show's closure and driven the proprietors into bankruptcy and a total loss of their original investment of $200,000.[67]

Coup was sued in a Cincinnati court and lost to a verdict of $40,000. But later, the plaintiffs' attorney, a Mr. Logan, claiming the evidence brought forward by his clients warranted a greater settlement, requested the original verdict be set aside and the claim for damages be increased to $300,000. Barnum was not served at that time. Forewarned of a subpoena, he managed to slip out of town by horse and carriage and drive eighteen miles, leaving the sheriff waiting at the wrong railway station. And, it was rumored, Barnum had been avoiding Cincinnati since that time.[68]

In their renewed suit the plaintiffs upped their losses, raising them to the aforementioned $300,000, stating that DeHaven alone had invested $210,000. They further charged Barnum and Coup of hiring twenty men at Ogdensburg to enter the employ of DeHaven and that "said emissaries did stab DeHaven, and so disable him that the dismemberment of the circus was inevitable."[69]

It is a fact DeHaven was attacked in Ogdensburg. On July 1, while he was standing in front of the Judson Bank Building, he was stabbed by Hugh Ferguson, a groom attached to the show. The culprit was quickly apprehended; but while being taken away by the police officers another employee set upon DeHaven, stabbing him again. The injuries were not fatal, however, and the victim made a relatively fast recovery.[70]

As one would expect, Barnum had much to say about the current claims of the plaintiffs. When encountered by a member of the Chicago *Inter-Ocean*, he responded, "I suppose you come about this law suit. Well, sir, just say for me that it is a gigantic swindle. It is done either to get money or a notoriety which will lead to money. It is a conspiracy. That's what it is, and nothing less." He went on to claim that when Haight and DeHaven owned the Great Eastern Circus, "representing itself as possessed of Barnumistic attractions," they "reaped a harvest of money." Then, in 1875, these "dizzy showmen and professional swindlers" (his words) secured copies of all of the Great Hippodrome bills and advertising paper from the printer, Sam Josephs, and began using it. Once it was discovered by him, along with the knowledge that his show was being superseded in towns, giving an impression that the Roman Hippodrome management was duplicating its attraction, Barnum set about warning the public of the imposters through display advertisements. The effect, he stated, caused DeHaven to request a meeting with Coup to arrange a settlement of the rivalry. A meeting was held in June of 1875, when an agreement was entered into stipulating no further infringement of the rights of the Barnum show would take place and no further prosecutions would be instituted. Shortly after the articles of agreement was established, the Racing Association broke up at Ogdensburg.[71]

Barnum went on to accuse the plaintiffs of attempting to have his train derailed, so great was their animosity toward him. As for the allegations and final judgment against Coup, he declared it was as absurd as it was false, a verdict given by "a put-up jury." The case was taken as far as the Supreme Court, where it remained until this present year of 1879. In an attempt to come to a conclusion, Barnum, the *Inter-Ocean* revealed, wanted the suit either tried or dismissed. A motion for dismissal was made and, in the first week of August, 1879, the judge issued an order to that effect. "Now, I have been advised to have them fellows arrested for malicious prosecution," Barnum told the reporter, "and I do not know but I shall."[72]

The final year of Barnum's "Greatest Show on Earth" under the management of the "Flatfoots" lost none of the elements that had made the show's reputation synonymous with its boastful title. The amusement level of the museum, menagerie, and ring performance throughout the years of

1876 to 1880 changed little. The organization, under the leadership of the aging management, held its own against the increased competition led by younger, energetic proprietors. "The character of Mr. Barnum's shows is so well understood that the better class of citizens patronize his entertainments," affirmed the Milwaukee *Sentinel.*[73]

The headliners of the 1880 circus were the Zulu warriors and Zazel, the human cannon ball, tight-rope performer, and aerialist. Both acts were brought to this country under the watchful eyes of Signor Farini. Guillermo Antonio Farini, whose real name was William Leonard Hunt, was actually born near Lockport, New York, in 1838. Possessing natural athletic ability, be began performing stunts on the wire very early in life. In 1860 he challenged Blondin on a crossing of Niagara Falls and followed through by walking the cable at a distance of 1,800, longer than previous Blondin crossings. He went to England five years later and began schooling a number of protégés. In 1877 he developed what is considered the first cannon ball act for one of them, Miss Rosa M. Richter, or as she was billed, Zazel. Because of Farini's reputation as a developer of spectacular acts, he is noted as a possible model for George du Maurier's character of Svengali in the novel *Trilby.*

The importation of the Zulu warriors was timely because disturbances in South Africa were frequently in the news. The English papers in particular were filled with letters and telegrams describing the conditions of affairs in Zululand up to the end of April and beyond. One correspondent asserted that the Zulu war was rapidly assuming the dimension of the Crimean war and perhaps outgrowing it. In support of this statement, the British army that was lined up on the Zulu frontier totaled some 30,000 men.

"ZAZEL!"

Zululand was a territory, situated on the Indian Ocean in the lower east portion of what is now South Africa. The British in an effort to create stability in the region, annexed the Transvaal in 1877; but border disputes between the Zulus and the Boers continued until on December 11, 1878, the British, seeking to protect their interests, presented demands amounting to an ultimatum to the Zulu chieftain. These were ignored and war followed. A British force totaling more than 1,200 men was almost annihilated at Isandhlwana on January 22, 1879, but on July 4 the British won a decisive battle at Ulundi. The Zulus admitted defeat and gave up the struggle.

Zulus were tribesmen of Bantu stock, well-proportioned, muscular, powerful, and active people above middle height, dependent for their sustenance both on the cultivation of millet and on cattle raising. Their homes were a framework of poles, beehive in form, thatched and plastered.

These huts are grouped together in a circular *kraal,* with the cattle in the center. Among other activities, they made millet beer, tanned hides, smelt iron, and wove baskets. The weapons they used were the assegai, knob-kirri, and shield.

Was this quartet of black men real Zulus? Probably. In any case, their ring performance was unique and exciting. It began with a demonstration of their skills in throwing a number of light, iron-tipped spears at a target, which generally had the audience seated in the section behind it somewhat edgy. They also performed a war dance, which was made quite impressive with their athletic figures dressed, or undressed, as they were with ostrich feathers on their headgear and more surrounding their unmentionables.

> The Zulus came dancing into the circle chanting their barbarous songs. They were savagely accoutred with assegais and shields. Their garbs, which were exceedingly scant, were decorated with ostrich feathers, as were their heads. Their forms were lithe, and as they threw their assegais, or spears, and pierced the target each time, one would imagine that they would prove tough customers to handle.[74]

One of their number disappeared at Detroit in May. He was found a few days later east of Windsor, Ontario, happy to be out of show business. D. S. Thomas, the Barnum show agent, accompanied by a sister of Zazel, who had learned to converse with the Zulus, went after him and, following some persuasion, returned him to the fold of his war dancing colleagues.

Sharing applause with the Africans was the daring feats of Zazel, while mading her American debut. For the first of a series of feats she ascended to a tight-wire, walked across it using a small parasol, but discarded it for her return. She next ascended to a trapeze and performed a number of exercises. Then she mounted a stationary platform from which she dove off head first and landed in a net below. For the finale she climb onto an elevated platform from which was suspended a large mortar or cannon-like contraption and into which she entered feet first. A fuse was lit from a torch held by Farini, causing the mortar to discharge Zazel and propel her through the air until she fell unharmed upon a net some distance away. "The sensation of witnessing this act is thrilling," the *Inter-Ocean* attendee wrote, "and those who doubt its wonderful actuality are advised to visit the tent to observe for themselves."[75] The Janesville *City Times* agreed:

> The series of remarkable feats that are displayed by this young lady are the same which attracted so much attention in London, Paris and New York. Her walk upon an almost invisible wire is a picture of beauty. One must imagine that she has wings. Her dive from the top of the canvas into the net fifty feet below is so graceful that it relieves the mind of all its fear for the personal welfare of the brave little gymnast. Her flight from the monster gun is effected so quickly that the audience have time hardly to realize that the report of the powder and the discharge of the female cannon ball has actually taken place.[76]

As in the past, the most affable D. S. Thomas was in charge of showing the members of the press about the show grounds. Prior to the matinee, he called upon them at their office with his carriage and personally drove them to the lot. There he guided them through the museum, where the human oddities were ready to be observed and interviewed, and on to the menagerie to be schooled on various progenies exhibited therein. One must speculate that there were handouts made plump with glowing phrases of the establishment, scripted by the circus writers in hopeful anticipation that they would be reproduced as news items on the following day. Scribes of the local papers rarely failed to mention the excursion:

> We went round with him yesterday in all the tents, side-shows and waiting rooms. To visit the latter place, as the boys and girls are buckling on their armor and sashes for the grand entrée, is indeed a prominent and most interesting feature of the display. It is here that

we see human nature to perfection. Here the clowns act natural, and the actors vie with each other in decorous action. Each animal knows its place, and when the bugle sounds the charge everything moves off systematically as clock work.[77]

The 1880 season opened for two weeks at the American Institute on the afternoon of April 8. The usual program consisted of a pre-show concert by Joseph Wither's band, followed by the grand entree, which echoed other years of Barnumania with the familiar walk-around by the artists and oddities—this year being Capt. Costentenus, Col. Goshen, tiny Nellie Keeler, Queen Mab, four Zulus, twenty-four ladies and gentlemen, and an assortment of animals.

An array of talented artists followed the Zulus and preceded Zazel on the program. R. M. Dockrill introduced his trained stallions Marmaluke and Pacha; Mlle. Leone rode a principal act, supported by the clowning of John Robinson; Herr and Mme. Martha Neygaard, making their American debut, worked their mounts through a double *manège* act; acrobatics and posturing were performed by the Nelson Family; Lizzie Marcellus rode a principal act to the clowning of J. McCarty; the Leotards executed more gymnastics; Orrin Hollis rode bareback as eight clowns cavorted at intervals; Nelson and sons returned to play violins while performing some difficult acrobatic feats; Emma Lake went through her *manège* routine; Mme. Nelson introduced a number of well trained doves which circled through the air and returned at her command, alighting on her shoulders and head and such other tricks; Mme. Dockrill performed her principal act; Charles White handled a couple of trained oxen, which knelt upon four legs, mounted pedestals, put one foot on an elevated post, stood with all feet on small stands, ascended and descended a small flight of double stairs, fired a pistol by pulling a string with their teeth, and played at seesaw; Signor Sebastian rode a bareback act and a carrying act with little

Louis; a horse and stag jumped over backs of other horses and other obstacles placed around the arena; there was *battoute* leaping by the company, which featured John Batcheller's double-somersault over several elephants; and finally, came the black Trakene stallions, introduced this season by R. M. Dockrill.

The wonderfully trained stallion, Salamander, which had been acquired from Germany's Circus Renz, galloped through a door panel encircled with exploding fireworks and jumped through a number of flaming hoops. At one performance an attendant erred by allowing a hoop to slip his grip, and the frightened horse ran off with a fiery necklace.

The incident prompted a quick complaint from the ever-watchful Henry Bergh, prominent and vocal member of New York's SPCA. He had been badgering Barnum for years about the treatment of animals in the ring, really since 1866 when the SPCA was first organized. Pressure from Bergh compelled the Barnum people to discontinue the act. Barnum reacted by challenging Bergh to meet him in the circus ring and respond to the explanations Barnum would give concerning the cruelty issue. Bergh accepted. Oh! this was a publicity windfall for Barnum, suckering his adversary into conflict on Barnum turf, in communion with an arena full of Barnum sympathizers. It was his metier, speechifying in the ring, as he had done over and over during the last decade, using his full catalog of self-serving adjectives.

On the date agreed to, the Coliseum, or rather the American Institute Building, was filled to capacity with patrons hungry to watch the rhetorical combat. Superintendent Hartfield, from the Society for the Prevention of Cruelty to Aminals, was in attendance, along with seven of his officers. Police Captain Gunner, the man who made out the report that forced the action, was there as well. And twenty policemen were positioned at selected stations around the ring. Then, when Orrin Hollis had finished his bareback riding exhibition, Barnum entered the ring to an outburst of applause. The cards had been stacked from the outset. When the applause and acclamation subsided, Barnum addressed the audience, submitting a lengthy and convincing defense.

Upon finishing, Barnum's soliloquy was received with tremendous cheering. The horse Salamander was then brought into the ring by Herr Nagaard, its trainer, and the fire hoops were lighted. Barnum ran his hand through the blaze, and then stepped through the flaming circle, hat in hand. Ten clowns performed a number of ludicrous antics through the hoops, and then the horse passed through without showing any signs of fear and without singeing a hair. Barnum then requested Superintendent Hartfield to walk through the still blazing hoops. Without hesitation he did so. He then stated that his superior, Mr. Bergh, had evidently made a mistake in the matter, that there was neither cruelty nor danger in the performance, and that the society had no cause for action. Salamander was free to go through his tricks again.

Almost everywhere the show went local voices offered the opinion that this was the best circus ever under the Barnum name. A typical assessment was expressed by a Janesville paper when it was stated that "the show is without doubt the best that Mr. Barnum has ever presented here, and deserves the patronage which it is receiving." Considering the quality of all the departments, this could very well be the truth. Lacking, when compared to other major circuses, were trained elephants. Although there were ten on the lot when the season started (one was "sent away" on August 14), they were not worked in the ring.

This was the longest and most profitable season for Barnum under "Flatfoot" management. After the New York City opening, the show went to Connecticut, Rhode Island, Massachusetts, New York State, Michigan, Indiana, Illinois,

Wisconsin, Minnesota, Iowa, Nebraska, Wyoming Territory, Colorado, Kansas, Missouri, back into Illinois and Indiana, Arkansas, Texas, Louisiana, and closed at Washington, Missouri; in all, comprising a total mileage of over 11,000.

The large attendance was commensurate of performance quality. A May 25 matinee in Detroit was said to have drawn 9,000 patrons and 13,000 for the night performance. At week at the lake front lot in Chicago, with two daily week-day showings plus three on Saturday, drew nearly 100,000 people. The total receipts for the season came to $573,692; of that, Barnum's share was $87,850.

IV
THE EMERGENCE OF
COOPER & BAILEY

T HE STAR OF JAMES A. BAILEY NOW begins its ascension. The young man, who had leased the concert privileges of Hemmings, Cooper & Whitby for the 1870 season, wasted no time in establishing his worth in the minds of the proprietors. After only one year with the concern, as a reward for his diligence and recognition of his true calling, Hemmings & Cooper paid him seventy dollars a week plus expenses as general agent—a general agent at barely twenty-three years of age.

The origins of James Ebenezer Cooper and James A. Bailey are somewhat similar. Cooper, the son of a blacksmith and wheelwright, was born in London on November 2, 1832. When he was less than a year old his parents migrated to the United States and settled in Philadelphia. After the death of his father, the enterprising young man, at age fifteen, went into business for himself, running a line of omnibuses from Philadelphia to Fox Chase. In time he sold the business and moved to Washington, D.C., where he started another omnibus line, a successful endeavor that led to his controlling nearly every route in the city. His entry into the circus business occurred in 1863 after he returned to Philadelphia.

The antecedents of the Cooper organization go as far back as 1860 when a partnership was formed by Dan Gardner and Richard Hemmings. The two made arrangements to

James E. Cooper

set up at a place on the outskirts of Philadelphia, known as Comac's Woods, the old Comac estate, at the end of the Tenth and Eleventh Street railway. The idea was to turn it into a summer resort with Gardner and Hemmings furnishing a circus to perform in the open and a daily tight-rope ascension to the top of a nearby building as an attraction to bring out the people. As this was the only resort of its kind in Philadelphia at the time, it was a big success. The circus did a phenomenal business up until the Fourth of July, at which time there were over 35,000 people on the grounds. But, as fortune would have it, on that day two rival volunteer fire companies were holding picnics. Toward evening things began to get heated between the intoxicated and combatant hosemen, then turned into a good, old fashion brouhaha. When the newspapers came out the next morning with headlines related to the riot, Comac's Woods was finished as a summer resort.

In the fall the company performed for five weeks at Gilmore's place on Walnut Street, Philadelphia, under the name of Gardner, Hemmings and Madigan. Their special feature for the engagement was Mons. Blondin, the great wire-walker and "Hero of Niagara," who proved to be an immense drawing card. After closing, they went to Baltimore and performed in the old Front Street Theatre and opened as Messrs. Madigan & Co., proprietors of The Great American Consolidated Circus.

The following year, 1861, John V. O'Brien rented horses to Gardner and Hemmings and went along as boss hostler to keep an eye on his property. In 1862 the show came out of the barns with nine baggage wagons, a new pole rig, a new bandwagon, and twenty-eight newly purchased government horses, the enlargement made possible by the addition of John O'Brien, who, as a silent partner held one-third interest in the organization. Cooper bought O'Brien's interest in the concern early in 1863, at which time the title was changed to Gardner, Hemmings & Cooper. Three years later, he acquired Dan Gardner's share of the show. In 1868, Harry Whitby was added and the title became Hemmings, Cooper & Whitby. In the fall of 1870, Whitby was shot and killed during a front-door riot in Mississippi, forcing anew a title change for the 1871 season, this time to Hemmings & Cooper.

Then, on February 20, 1872, Richard Hemmings sold his interest in the show to Cooper. Hemmings had recently married and wanted out of the responsibility of management. This year George Middleton and Bailey leased the privileges on the show—sideshow, concert, and candy stand—at $625 a week for the first twenty weeks and $425 a week for the next ten weeks, with a $2,000 payment in advance. If a thirty week season was not completed, the contract stated, a portion of the advance money would be returned. Hemmings & Cooper were to supply the cost of transportation for the concert people and furnish four musician for it. As part of the agreement, Bailey was to be an advertising consultant at no extra pay.[1]

The show went out as James E. Cooper's International Circus for the 1873 season. Cooper, who was then a three-quarter owner (another quarter was held by Robert S. Hood), in a move to keep Bailey within the organization, sold him a one-quarter interest for $10,000, with $1,000 as a down payment and the remainder to be paid over a period of months through six notes. Bailey was to devote his work to the enterprise at no salary, but would receive his share of the profits. He would get no capital stocks until the notes were paid off.[2] Unaffected by the addition to ownership, Bailey and Middleton retained the concert and sideshow privileges.

The show under James A. Bailey's first co-management was modest in size. It carried about 100 employees,

156 horses, and eighteen wagons and featured a two tent system, which allowed the patrons to visit the menagerie and museum without having to attend the performance. The very prosperous season was closed at Natchez, Mississippi, on December 14. It was the original intention to continue into February, but medical problems among the horses forced the termination. The outfit was then shipped by boat to winter quarters in Louisville, Kentucky.

The circus, still under Cooper's name, started the 1874 season from there with a performing roster that would not have been recognized as "first team all-Americans." The featured acts were Mme. DeGranville, the iron-jawed lady; Joseph Tinkham, hurdle rider; and Andy Spear, trick clown.[3] Certainly, names belonging in the second rank, as indicated by the following from the *Weekly Kansas Chief.*

> Hard times showed themselves on the occasion of the Circus, Tuesday. The jam that a circus usually brings to Troy, was not visible. There was a considerable attendance, but not as on former occasions.... Some of the circus performances were tolerably good but as a general thing they were ordinary—not as good as the average circus—while the stale and tedious wit of the clowns was fearful.... To sum up, the show wasn't much to brag of.[4]

Cooper, Bailey & Co.—Bailey's participation within the firm had increased—took a giant leap forward for the 1876 season. James E. Cooper was still the general manager of the show, assisted by Charles Kidder. Robert S. Hood was the treasurer and part owner (on August 14, 1877, however, Hood sold his interest to Bailey for $1,000 cash and seven promissory notes of unstated amount). The privileges were held by George W. Middleton and William H. Gardner.

Expansion necessitated converting to rail travel. The management claimed the acquisition of forty-three show-owned cars. The main tent was a 125 foot round top with a fifty foot middle piece, which seated 6,000 spectators. The

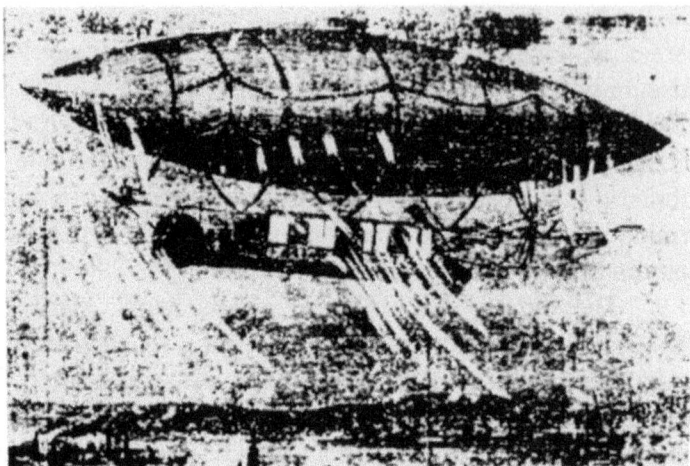

menagerie and museum tent was a 70 foot with three 30 foot middles. The dressing tent was a 50 foot round top.

The outside attraction was somewhat unique. Cooper, Bailey & Co. obtained the sole right to exhibit Prof. O. A. Hutchinson's "Flying Ship of the Air" to be shown in operation daily. The flying vehicle was a balloon, long and pointed at each end, resembling a flying torpedo, from which a gondola was attached. Like the ordinary balloon, it relied on existing air currents for movement, but could be steered in any direction by the inventor's use of propellers mounted on each side. In all probability, the airborne attraction was limited to the early weeks of the season; we have found no reference to it in later newspaper accounts or advertisements.

The show was a decided improvement over previous years. It was headlined by the great equestrian James Robinson and sons Clarence and Eugene.[5] The route book listed fifteen acts in the program including the grand entrée. The menagerie was heavily promoted in an attempt to keep within reach of the Barnum and Forepaugh shows. The advertising claimed to have the only four living sea lions, the only baby sea lions, and the only living giraffe in America. There were five trained elephants, baby camels, Zebras driven in harness, sixty Shetland ponies, buffaloes, and, so it was advertised, fifty cages of wild animals. A tiny elephant, Topsy, only thirty-eight inches high was newly purchased.

The season got off to a banner start. Cooper, Bailey & Co.'s Great International 10 Allied Shows and Howes' Great London Circus had both wintered at the Fair Grounds in St. Louis. Each management desired to begin the season around the same dates; so, rather than waste their resources in opposition, the two companies combined for a big opening week beginning April 17, with three exhibitions given daily. The double street procession was said to have taken two hours to pass a given point. This resulted in turn-away business for almost every performance.

Bailey was so concerned about the season, it being a year of national celebration, fearing that many Americans would be saving their money for a trip to the Philadelphia Centennial Exposition, that he decided to tour the circus westward. This selection was mainly responsible for the shift to rail travel.

It has been written that a decision to transport the circus to Australia was made before the season began. The wealth "down under" and the potential within the region was an incentive for going; and much was made of the Australian trip in advertising throughout the season. But in reading Crowley's account in the Cooper & Bailey Australian route book, the weighty final determination was not made until the circus arrived in San Francisco in early September. The management discussed the possibility of success with various show people who had experienced the journey, before making the final commitment to go. "Consultations were had," he wrote, "and yet none knew their results until late in

the following month, when it became known that the show
was to be equipped for a voyage across the Pacific."

The successful western trek can be attributed to a
well organized advertising department. James Bailey was, of
course, the general advance manager. He was assisted by
Charles W. Fuller, general agent and railroad contractor; J.
B. Gaylord, advertising agent; Claude Williams, advance
press agent; R. G. Ball, contracting agent; J. W. Heidler,
agent at large; Edward Gaylord, excursion agent. J. J.
Showles was chief in command of the crew of ten billposters; William Martin, the advance courier distributor; W. G.
Crowley, the press agent back with the show.

The itinerary was well planned, towns carefully selected with conditions of crops, manufacturing, and prosperity being thoroughly researched. After leaving St. Louis, the
show traveled through Missouri, Kansas, Nebraska, Iowa,
Illinois, back into Iowa, Minnesota, Wisconsin, Nebraska,
Colorado, Wyoming Territory, Utah, Nevada, and California,
closing on October 21 at Oakland. The travel mileage for
the 187 day season amounted to a total of 12,977.

Before leaving the middle states Cooper, Bailey &
Co. encountered plenty of opposition. There were eight other
circuses traversing the area through Iowa, Minnesota, Wisconsin, and Illinois. Old John Robinson was encountered at
Burlington, Iowa, and Canton, Illinois. L. B. Lent's, the
Sells Bros.', Dan Castello's, Burr Robbins', and Howes'
Great London all felt the heat from Bailey's advance crew of
special agents and aggressive bill posters. In the 1876 route
book Crowley wrote that his show gave no ground. If other
shows were nearby they were heavily papered. "Agent after
agent was sent to the front and gang after gang of bill posters
assailed the enemy until they were beaten and buried beneath
the paper of the Great International." James A. Bailey was

showing the circus world that, although small in stature, he was a Goliath when it came to a fight for territory.

We learn something about Bailey's advance advertising from a clipping out of a Clinton, Iowa, newspaper dated June 12. There were 1,040 lineal feet of billboards occupied in that place in addition to ads in the local paper. The Sterling City Band, presumably a local organization, was hired to ballyhoo Clinton and surrounding communities. The band mobilized in an elegant wagon that was accompanied by a moving billboard twenty feet long and twelve feet high, which announced the coming of the circus. The total cost for advertising in Clinton was estimated at $500.

Large billboards were erected in Topeka, Kansas, for the May 11 date, as described by the *Commonwealth*:

> The billboards on which are displayed the circus posters continue to draw large and admiring audiences. It is believed there was not a minute between sunrise and sunset on Sunday last that some man, woman or child was not standing in front of the big board just south of the State printing office.[6]

The company was well received by the press everywhere, who consistently praised the management on quality and respectability—free of courseness and vulgarity. This would be an identifying feature of a Bailey-owned operation.

The circus arrived in San Francisco on September 6, whereupon a portion of the stock was auctioned off before leaving for Australia.[7] The preparations for going on such a long and unfamiliar trip required careful planning and a sizeable outlay of capital. It was important to secure the commitment of the star performer, James Robinson, for the necessary months away from the United States, as well as others in the company. The whole outfit had to be stripped to the utmost economy and efficiency without weakening performance and the physical functioning of the organization.

One can easily imagine the excitement of the entire company as time neared for departure. Crowley's route book reveals the true nature of the anxious leave-taking festivities, or in his words, the "great goings on in 'Frisco' just before it started."

> The halls of the great International Hotel resounded with the voices of the gang and their friends, for a few nights before the day of departure. There were gatherings, and hurrying to and fro. Hundreds of anecdotes are still in circulation relative to the last few days and how they were passed. There was the social gathering at the Elks' rooms, the Sunday evening before the departure, when the safety of those going out upon the sea was fervently asked for by a member; there was the wild hurrah of the Presidential election the day before; and the "god-speed-you-all" at Colonel Hayes' rooms the night before the company left. Then, who can forget the articles purchased for the voyage; the preventatives against sea-sickness; for the removal of bile before the waves forcibly removed it, etc., etc.?

The circus departed from San Francisco for Australia on November 8, 1876 aboard the *City of Sydney*, leaving the controversy over the presidential election to be sorted out by those who remained behind. It would be away for two full years. It's home-coming would mark the new mission of Cooper & Bailey, that of becoming the most competitive and powerful arenic organization in the country.

&

Cooper, Bailey & Co. returned to the United States in December of 1878, the worse for wear for their two years away. The tour of Australia and the Far East had been profitable, but the decision to go to South America was an undoing. The circus arrived home with nothing to show for their absence and with many of the animals lost on the high seas from a stormy passage.

But something fortuitous occurred at this point to alter the course of ill luck. James Reilly, the silent partner and patient mortgage holder of Howes' Great London for the past two years, decided to recover some of his losses by selling the show. He offered James Bailey the outfit on credit for a bargain price of $23,000, the debt to be paid off over an undisclosed period of time. Bailey's wise acceptance led to the formation of "The Great Allied Shows."

With the marriage of these two circuses, Cooper and Bailey were equipped to take on all comers. The acquisition of the still astonishing Howes Golden Chariots made their street procession the finest in the country. Their elephant herd of ten ($100,000 worth) was one of the largest. And alongside their own circus title were the names of both Great London and Sanger, for the show was universally billed as "The Great London Circus, Sanger's Royal British Menagerie, with Cooper, Bailey & Co.'s Famous International

Allied Shows." The name of Howes was missing, probably
discarded for legal reasons; but the Sanger name was retained, secured by the vastness of the Atlantic Ocean. In his
memoirs, Sir George Sanger claimed he never got paid for its
use after the Howes family relinquished the show.

What is more, there was a heightened public confi-
dence in the national economy. Secretary of the Treasury,
John Sherman, had accumulated around $200 million in gold
reserve, confirming the government's ability to redeem its
currency. Greenbacks had reached their face value in gold
for the first time since 1862, leading to an enactment by
Congress that made the outstanding ones a permanent part of
the currency. Circuses would do well.

Bailey's billing was lavish. "Two Shows! A Double
Circus! Two Menageries!" it read, "Nine Foreign Artists!
Lighted by Electricity! 168,000 Yards of Canvas! Seven
Golden Chariots! 35 Cages, Dens and Corralls of Rare and
Curious Animals!"

The advertising department was powerful and experienced, with James A. Bailey, a man of great ability and
tireless energy, chief in command of everything ahead of the
show. He put together a crew of able assistants and spared
no expense in announcing the Cooper & Bailey arrival.
Posters, programs, dodgers, hangers, letters, lithographs, and
newspaper displays were used without limit. Charles W.
Fuller was the general agent; John W. Hamilton the advance
press agent; D. K. Townsend and Henry Hedges, contracting
agents; Charles Whitney and Leon A. Jones, excursion
agents; and Charles Bernard the stereopticon agent. The two
advertising cars were supervised by Col. T. H. Toole and
Samuel H. Joseph, and Crete Pulver was manager of the
middle brigade.

The names of stereopticon agents have been included
on circus rosters at various times before this. The following

is an example of their labors. Topeka, Kansas, was favored with a free exhibition on July 24 outside of the Tefft House from a large screen stretched across the front of it. It is quite probable that the lecturer for these illustrations positioned himself on a balcony or in an open window above the heads of the crowd.

> The Great London Circus, illustrated by over 200 beautiful pictures, brilliantly illuminated by calcium lights. The vast pavilions, the menagerie, acrobat riders, gymnasts, the grand street procession and everything of interest pertaining to the Great Show placed before your eyes in a realistic manner. Amusing and interesting to both old and young. Something worth seeing. Don't miss it. Remember to-night. Free to all.[8]

The outstanding street procession that heralded the show's arrival was well advertised in advance. "Magnificent Pageant on the Public Street!" "At 9:00 a.m.," the bills announced, "Our Unrivalled Street Display Will Take Place." "On the morning of the exhibition the Grandest, Longest, Most Resplendent and Original Spectacular and Mardi Gras Public Pageant will pass along the principal thoroughfares, exposing to the public countless novelties never before held in a similar display." How could anyone resist?

They didn't. Such an event in Detroit was given high approval, as expressed in the *Free Press:* "The principal features of the pageant were two fine brass bands, a steam piano, ten elephants, a long procession of cages on wheels containing the smaller animals belonging to the menagerie, a drove of Shetland ponies, gaily appareled cavaliers, comical masqueraders, and stupendous chariots, all of which excited the shrill admiration of juvenile Detroit and the calmer approval of the many thousands of older persons to whom the coming of 'the circus' is an event that sets the blood bounding with the recollections of youthful happiness."[9]

People came from every direction, flocking into town to witness the great parade, some arriving as early as 5:00 a.m. Before 9:00 the streets were thronged with anxious onlookers. The procession made an appearance around 9:30 or 10:00, headed by the tally-ho coach and followed by an awesome visual spectacle and the resounding music of the two bands. A circus orator passed along the line of gazers, calling their attention to the free exhibition on the show grounds at the close of the parade. Thereupon, the crowd relocated to where the big tents were spread to watch the daring tight-rope performer make her ascension.[10]

Cooper & Bailey's Great London of 1879 was the first organization to make use of a system of electric lighting. It was Bailey who saw the possibilities of this novelty and had the courage to introduce it when others felt it might prove a failure. He made much of it in the advertising and charged extra for the public to get a view of the unique generator.

This great innovation and the accompanying lamps were manufactured by the Charles F. Brush Co. of Cleveland, Ohio, at a cost to the circus management of $15,000, which included the exclusive right of use under canvas. The system was run by a thirty-five horse power engine with an armature that averaged 750 revolutions per minute and which powered twelve carbon-pencil burners. The illumination was very intense, flooding the spaces with an extreme whiteness in contrast to the yellow, smokey, flickering jets of other circuses. In the main tent, ground glass globes were applied to soften the glare of the six lights; but the three lighting instruments in each of the other two tents were not shielded.[11] The whole electrical system was under the supervision of John Sherman.

The generating plant, the largest of its kind yet made, was designed for the necessary portability of a traveling circus. It rested on a large wagon, especially constructed for that purpose, on the rear of which was a calliope. Power was conducted from the machine to the lamps by several cables made of seven strands of No. 16 copper wire, covered with a layer of gutta-percha, a tough plastic substance from latex, over which was a layer of plaited cotton. From one to seventeen lamps could be lit by simply varying the speed of the engine, and each one could be controlled independently—turned on and off—without interrupting the use of the others.[12]

Another innovation this year was the nocturnal street parade which occurred in the larger cities—Philadelphia, Chicago, and St. Louis. In these places, preceding advertisements announced that no shows would be given on Monday afternoon and evening, because of the "Grand Mammoth Midnight Spectacular Street Parade." This cut the circus

income to a five-day week. As a means of compensating for
the lost Monday, a third performance, with doors opening at
9:00 a.m., was given daily in these cities.

"Midnight" may have been a misnomer, however,
for we learn from a Chicago correspondent that in that city
on June 16 the procession set out at 8:00 p.m. from its lake
front lot en route to the down town area where a large and
expectant crowd awaited. The spectacle was preceded by
armored knights, some fifty in number, bearing torches emit-
ting a brilliance of red and green. The gilded display wagons
scattered along the gaudy caravan were aglow from calcium
lights, where, from their highest seats, more torch bearers
manipulated red, blue, and green fire and occasionally sent
up Roman candles. The ornate cage wagons, some of them
open, were illuminated with Chinese lanterns. The caparisoned horses and the colorfully attired equestrians and elephants were also accentuated by the glare of torches and calcium lights. Bringing up the rear was the grandest con-
veyance of them all, the Golden War Chariot of India, surmounted by its life-size replica of an elephant. Directly following, and at the very end of the procession, was the calliope—its accompanying steam machine making a constant
wake of sparks to add to the fireworks—belching forth a ca-
cophony of sonorous notes.[13]

The elephant herd was a big attraction and, at this
time, a yardstick by which people judged the size and quality
of the show inside the tents. This year, under the supervision
of George Arstingstall, it was made up of Chieftain, Mandarin (Mandrie), Princess, Mama, and Victoria (Hebe), coming
with the acquisition of the Great London show, and Titania,
Khedive, Romeo, Juliet, and Prince (the clown) from the
former International Allied Shows. The combined weight
was reported at 53,117 pounds. The number was the same as
rival Adam Forepaugh's, although Forepaugh boasted of

twelve. There were claims of having the only ten performing elephants in the ring at one time, of the only team of three and four elephants to harness, of the ten in drilled military maneuvers, of the only trotting elephant harnessed to a sulky, of the only clown elephant, of three teetering elephants, and of the only herd consisting of all species and sexes—African, Asian, Indian, Ceylonese. Then, by September—will the good fortune never end?—the Great London bills were announcing, "The Female Elephant Victoria, About to Become a Mother, will be on Exhibition daily without extra charge."

The astute management demonstrated a sensitivity to audience comfort and enjoyment. Within the main tent, 250 feet in length, there were 2,000 reserved seats, carpeted and with backs, at a cost of 25¢ extra (at times they were advertised as "special folding opera chairs with foot and back rests"). The annoying vendors of lemonade and confectionery during the performance was entirely eliminated. In the center of the menagerie tent, for the amusement of the children, was an immense corral in which twenty-seven ponies and four little donkeys were kept. And, of course, improved illumination within the tents was created by the new electric generator. There were generally two performances daily, at 2:00 and 7:00 p.m. The usual hour was allotted for browsing the menagerie before the start of the arenic activity.

This was still a one-ring circus, but the company of performing artists was strong. Charles Fish and Adelaide Cordona were the star equestrians, well supported by riders Frank Melville, and William Dutton. Nat Austin was the equestrian director and Robert Ellingham the ringmaster.[14] Four African lions were performed by Theodore Ferris and four Bengal tigers by Alfred Still. At the start of the season, Ferris, fairly new to the business, had been working with the beasts throughout a two-week period of instruction at winter quarters by George W. Johnston. The tigers and their trainer

James L. Hutchinson

were brought over from Liverpool in 1871 with Howes' Great London. It has been said that in dealing with the cats Still used only a whip of stiff rawhide without a loaded handle. He never cut their claws and never used an iron bar or club on them.

James L. Hutchinson, who started as a canvasman in the early 1860s, was proprietor of the privileges—sideshow, concert, and candy stand.[16] This was the same man who made a fortune for Barnum, not to mention a sizeable amount for himself, by selling the autobiography out of a wagon when Barnum first entered the circus business. Within less than two years he would become the matchmaker the brings Barnum and Bailey together.

The season was highly profitable. On opening night of the Washington, D.C., stand (April 29-30), 6,000 people filled the tent. The ticket window was closed before the performance began and many were turned away. In Allegheny City, just across the river from Pittsburgh, the tent was jammed for the opening afternoon and at night some 3,000 were refused tickets. It was estimated that nearly 30,000 people attended during the two days there. At Chicago on June 18, the tent for the evening performance was so full, estimated at nearly 8,000 in the audience, that the doors had to be closed some fifteen minutes before the show was to begin and a thousand people were turned away. It was reported in the *Inter-Ocean* on June 20, "Another army of disappointed people applied for admission at the circus last evening, only to find that there was no room left for them." The crowd inside surpassed that of the evening before because the accommodations had been increased by adding seats closer to the ring. Even so, more people were admitted than there were seats for them. This kind of public response induced the management to telegraph their tent maker in New York to order another fifty-foot middle piece of canvas, which increased the seating by 2,000.[15] Two extra middle pieces carried with the show were put in at Minneapolis, Omaha, Jacksonville, Cedar Rapids, Quincy, St. Louis, Ft. Worth, Dallas, and a few other places.

At the Baltimore stand beginning April 23 the street procession was delayed until around 2:00 p.m. and the matinee was cancelled because the show was late in arriving from Wilmington. The lot there was practically a mire, to the extent that the poles, seats, tenting, etc., had to be carried off by hand because loaded wagons would not have been able to move through it. To make matters worse, the Baltimore lot at Charles Street, near Biddle, was too small. The museum tent was not erected at all and a middle piece had to be left out of the main tent. Still, a crowd of 4,000 attended the night performance, with the reserve seat section occupied by people "one usually sees at the Academy of Music rather than at a circus."[16]

Bailey became an equal partner in the Great International late in the season. He purchased Robert Hood's share for $1,000 down and seven promissory notes for undisclosed amounts to pay off the remainder. The 1879 route book states that the transaction occurred at Clinton, Illinois, but this is an error. The company did not perform there in 1879, but was at Clinton, Iowa, on the 23rd of September.

This year the show traversed a route that totaled 10,928 miles. After finishing off in the East at the end of April, it moved through Pennsylvania, into Ohio, Michigan, Wisconsin, Minnesota, Iowa, Missouri, Kansas, Nebraska, back into Iowa, Illinois, Missouri, Kansas, and then into Texas, Arkansas, and Missouri, closing at Piedmont, Missouri, on December 1. The outfit was then dead-headed the 1,100 miles back to winter quarters in Philadelphia, ending the lengthy circuit with a profit of around $500,000.

1880 was a presidential election year. Although there was controversy again, and a surprise nomination of James A. Garfield, and a summer marred by electioneering scandal, the circus season for Cooper & Bailey was even more astonishing than the previous one. In Hartford, Connecticut, a correspondent observed that the "street pageant was the most gorgeous ever witnessed" in that community and was enjoyed by thousands of delighted spectators, and at the performances thousands were turned away.[17] The year was highlighted by the birth of the so-called "first baby elephant born in civilization." A second ring was incorporated. The electric light plant was still an inviting curiosity. The herd of elephants had increased to twelve. Cooper, Bailey & Co. had become the largest and most vibrant show on the road.

During the winter lay-off, everything connected with the show was thoroughly renovated. Cages were repainted and re-gilded, six new cage tableaux and a bandwagon built, harnesses and caparisons for the horses newly purchased.

The show bills and the newspaper cuts were newly designed. Eighty-two different lithographs were prepared. Advertising car #1 was installed with thirty chime bells, the largest one weighing 442 pounds; car #2 with a steam calliope. The main tent was a 180 foot round top with three 50 foot middle pieces. There were separate pavilions for menagerie and museum. Three trains carried the show, including three cars for the advance, four palace sleepers, and fifty-five other coaches owned by the proprietors.

The menagerie was enlarged by the addition of two elephants, two large polar bears, a number of sea lions, a hippopotamus, and a variety of birds and reptiles. There were thirty-two cages. Stewart Craven spent the winter months in Philadelphia training the twelve-elephant herd in military drill and improving the five-pyramid performance. There was also an elephant taught to walk the tight-rope and one was schooled to act a clown. The master trainer called his efforts "superior to anything of the kind yet seen."[18]

The season opener was in Philadelphia on Easter Monday, April 12. Cooper, Bailey & Co.'s Great London combined with the Great Forepaugh Show, the two august rivals coming together for a two-week stand. Both shows wintered in Philadelphia, so it is logical they both would open their season there and do it about the same time. Rather than oppose each other, playing day-and-date, why not combine and share the returns? Then, too, there is another point to be considered. Was this a tactic to intimidate the P. T. Barnum outfit?

The two shows also united in forming a mammoth torch light parade on Saturday, April 10. Together, there were 400 horses, thirty elephants and thirty camels represented. Twelve hundred torches were carried by as many men, making the street as light as day. Along the route fireworks were constantly set off. There were knights in armor, ladies on horseback, several bands, cages, and tableau cars. In all, it surpassed any such effort ever attempted in the Quaker City. Members of the press partook of hospitality by the two managements at the Girard House, from which they were able to observe the great spectacle as it passed by—that is, those who were able and willing to desert the bar for the necessary amount of time.

It was an exciting event for the Philadelphia public to see the combined talent of these two great circuses performing in two rings simultaneously. With the number of available acts and with two weeks to present them, there was a change of program throughout the run. And with action in both rings, the artists of the two shows were squared off in a friendly rivalry.

The Forepaugh people featured the bareback and six-horse riding of Frank Melville, the somersault riding of Wooda Cook, the aerial feats of George Loyal and Mlle. Zuila, as well as Richard and Elvira Hemmings, Jennie Ewers, Louise Boshell, Clarinda Lowande, and Harry Lamkin.

In the Cooper & Bailey ring there was the bareback riding of Charles Fish, the hurdle riding of Linda Jeal, the exciting equestrienne feats of Adelaide Cordona, and the arenic adventures of William Dutton, William H. Batcheller, Awati Katnoshin, the Lawrence Sisters, Crossley & Elder, the Davene Family, Jeronimo Bell, and the Herbert Brothers.

What an event! It was unanimous among visiting showmen that this was the greatest aggregate of circus acts ever brought together under a single canvas. What could Barnum be thinking?

The run closed on April 24 and the Forepaugh troupe opened at Wilmington, Delaware, on the 26th and Cooper & Bailey at Trenton, New Jersey, on the same date. Their cooperative performing at an end, the rivalry between them continued. For example, in the middle of June the Cooper &

Bailey advance crew billed Cleveland extensively, even though the circus was not scheduled to arrive until September. Within a month the Forepaugh crew came in and covered the billboards with ads for their August appearance. Every store window, express wagon, dray, omnibus, and streetcar carried an announcement. It seemed to be a contest as to which circus could spent the most on promotion.

Most important was the birth of the baby elephant, born at 2:30 a.m. on March 10 at the Cooper & Bailey Philadelphia winter quarters. The infant was called Columbia, but would be advertised at various times as America or Young America. It may also have privately answered to Lily, after the name of Stewart Craven's wife.

At that time it weighed 213½ pounds and measured three feet tall at the highest point from the ground, overall resembling the form of a mature specimen. The parents were a pair of Ceylon elephants, Mandrie and Hebe. Mandrie was 26 years old and weighed about 8,000 pounds. Hebe was 23 and weighed in at 7,020. The affectionate pair had not been separated since leaving their native country.

Both were part of the herd that was imported in 1871 when Elbert Howes was sent to Ceylon on an animal expedition. Their temperaments, however, were quite different. According to George N. Bates, who was a member of Barnum's elephant department for thirty years or more, Hebe, whose name was later changed to Babe, "was the prettiest elephant in the country and never really hurt anyone, except once.... Even the best of them are not trustworthy." On the other hand, "Mandarin was the worst elephant ever brought to this country. He would fairly eat a man alive." Unfortunately, in later years the newly born developed her father's disposition and had to be killed.

The birth cannot be attributed to the wisdom or foresight of the Cooper & Bailey organization. It was, rather, a

213 pound bundle of good fortune. When they took possession of the Great London from Parks, Davis, and Dockrill
after that partnership dissolved in late 1878 and the elephant
herd came with the purchase, no one had any knowledge that
one of its number was pregnant and would, within a year,
present the owners with a mine of golden publicity.

The question of why this particular mating was successful when, it is assumed, throughout the preceding years
that no other elephant had been born in captivity was plausi-
bly explained at the time by Stewart Craven. He pointed out
that conditions of menagerie life had changed markedly in
the recent years. Before rail travel the tenting season was
long and tiring, with the elephants having to walk from one
town to the next. They were not given winter surroundings
suitable for proper recuperation before having to return to
summer touring. They were exposed to severe weather quite
different from that of their natural habitat. It had been but
of recent years that they were kept together in herds and the
sexes allowed to mingle because prior to the 1870s the exhibition of only one or two elephants was deemed sufficient
for any single menagerie. The species were easily frightened
and at the most insignificant things. Now, with greater understanding and concern, they were being kept in surroundings beneficial to their health and happiness—more nutri-
tiously fed, more warmly quartered during the winter layoff,
guarded against unsettling interference, integrated into a herd
situation, and, to assure their endurance, were walked only in
the street processions.[19]

Much was made of the elephant's fortuitous birth. It
was a Cooper, Bailey & Co. claim and a universal assump-
tion that this was the first elephant to be born in the Western
World since the days of the Roman Empire. The thousands
of sheets of advertising induced an enormous public curiosity because of this. To this day it is generally accepted as

fact. But the reader will recall an earlier recounting of the birth of a baby elephant at St. Joseph, Missouri, when in 1875 the Howes' Great London circus was exhibiting in the West. This short-lived infant, which was to be named St. Joseph, may very well have been sired by the same parents as little Columbia.

It is curious that the two leading elephant trainers of that day, Stewart Craven and George Arstingstall have never commented about the inconsistency of these events. Arstingstall was with Howes' Great London the season following the birth of the former and both men were on hand for the birth of the latter. They certainly must have had knowledge of the two occurrences.

The birth of the elephant was followed by a national excitement. Newspapers and journals made much of it in picture and in story. Bailey went all out in billing the show. No less than fourteen advertising agents, newspaper writers, and designers of printing were busy in Philadelphia during the winter preparing for the summer publicity blitz. It was estimated that lithographs contracted from Strobridge & Co. and show printing from Russell, Morgan & Co. would amount to $50,000. Additional work was being done by James Reilly's printing house in New York City and the Courier's Company in Buffalo.

All this commotion was not lost on P. T. Barnum. At a moment of desperation, he sent a wire to Bailey, offering to buy the elephant for $100,000. Bailey refused the offer and, once in Barnum show territory, papered every space available with a reproduction of Barnum's telegram headed by "What Barnum Thinks of Our Baby Elephant," beating Barnum at his own game. "I found that I had at last met foemen 'worthy of my steel,'" Barnum wrote in his autobiography, "and pleased to find comparatively young men with a business talent and energy approximating of my own."[20]

Coming with my own Thirty-Four Palace-Built Cars, (equal in length to fifty ordinary cars,) forming the finest private built equipage in America.

THE WORLD'S WONDER LATELY ADDED, THE BULL OR BLUE HAIRY ELEPHANT, "ALBERT EDWARD." The Only One of the Kind Ever Captured.

A Curious Little Creature, the Nursing Elephant, "Chicago," Born at Germantown, Pa., Feb. 22d, 1877.

The Only Group of 5 Performing Elephants

[Owned by any one man in America.]

THAT BABY ELEPHANT.

Only Show in Maine this Summer.

OH! THAT PRECIOUS BABY!

Bath, Thursday, June 24, 1880.

THOUSANDS OF PEOPLE TURNED AWAY AT EACH PERFORMANCE!

Electric Blaze of Enthusiasm from Philadelphia to New England.

Such Demonstrations of Delight and such a Thorough Awakening
Never Before Heard of!

LOOK FOR IT | First Time of any BABY ELEPHANT!
First Time of any ELECTRIC LIGHT!
First Time of the ONLY 15 ELEPHANTS!

Positively the VERY BEST SHOW IN THE WORLD.

GREAT LONDON CIRCUS

AND

Sangers' Royal British Menagerie,

UNITED WITH THE TEN ALLIED SHOWS.

COOPER, BAILEY & Co., Sole Owners.

Only Great Confederation of Standard Exhibitions in the World.

First Baby Elephant Born in Civilization.

Again in 1880 the advance department headed by Bailey was manned by a crew of astute and experienced advertisers. Charles Fuller, as in 1879, was General Director; Joel W. Warner, General Manager; W. W. Durand, Publication Director; John W. Hamilton, Special Advance Manager; R. G. Ball, Contracting Agent; Samuel H. Joseph, Special Agent; J. A. Wood, Excursion Agent; H. C. Hedges, Mail Agent; G. A. Bernard, Stereopticon Agent; Matt Leland and Crete Pulver, Managers of the two advertising cars. In all, an aggregate of fifty-four men were employed in the advance, including agents, managers, superintendents, lithographers, bill posters, distributors, etc.

The advertising budget was immense, what with a heaven sent baby elephant to publicize and with two formidable competitors like P. T. Barnum's and Adam Forepaugh's circuses to do battle with. Perhaps for the first time by any such show a crayon artist, George M. Tuttle, and a soap artist, Lambert Hayman, were employed to go in advance as part of Advertising Car No. 2 to place pictures of the baby elephant on any and all available sidewalks and windows.

Fighting the opposition wars meant buying and posting more lithographs, composing and printing "rat sheets," contracting additional newspaper space, and billing much farther in advance of the performance dates than normal. Advance manager, John W. Hamilton, was especially vigorous in combating the Cooper & Bailey arenic rivals. According to the route book, he "worked with a will throughout the fight, and to his untiring zeal much of the victory is due."

New England and other near-by eastern states were considered Barnum's exclusive territory, where encroachment by other shows meant a battle. Cooper & Bailey, emboldened by their "baby elephant" advantage, put on the gloves and waded into the fray. Their advertising crews moved into Barnum's sacred East, billing their show in advance of his with posters struck up like this:

THERE WILL BE NO PERFORMANCE IN BRIDGEPORT
UNTIL MAY 10
BY THE GREAT LONDON SHOW

"The result of this final move," recalled Richard F. "Tody" Hamilton, "was to drive Barnum out of New England, leaving the territory to the undisputed possession of his rival."[21]

Barnum insisted that his circus was still the largest and best in the world:

So late in 1880, no traveling show in the world bore any comparison with my justly-called "Greatest Show on Earth".... The cost of one of their shows was from twenty thousand to fifty thousand dollars, while mine cost millions of dollars. Their expenses were three hundred to seven hundred dollars per day, while mine were three thousand dollars per day.[24]

He was wrong. Yes, Barnum's "Greatest Show on Earth," no matter how worthy, had become the "second banana" to Cooper & Bailey's Great London Circus and Allied Shows.

EPILOGUE:
MR. BAILEY AND MR. BARNUM

AMES COOPER RETIRED FROM THE circus business in October of 1880. This was revealed in a single line in the New York *Clipper* of August 21, stating that Bailey had purchased Cooper's interest in the Great London, the change of ownership to be affected on October 30. Cooper was said to have received $40,000 for his share of the firm.

It was announced only a few weeks later that Barnum had bought out the "Flatfoots" and formed a partnership with Bailey and James L. Hutchinson. Hutchinson was offered a cash free interest in the organization if he could induce Bailey into partnership; and, as it appears, he was successful. The deal Barnum made was similar to what he had had with the "Flatfoots." He retained fifty percent of the stock and each of his partners held twenty-five percent (Hutchinson's twenty-five percent seems excessive for someone who was only a deal-maker). For his share Barnum contributed his name and his show property; Bailey chipped in his holdings of Cooper, Bailey & Co. plus $7,500 more in cash. The capital assets came to $200,000. Different from earlier contracts, Barnum did not insist on a yearly bonus for the use of his famous name.

Further, it was suggested that the shows of Cooper, Bailey & Co. and of P. T. Barnum might combine to give a series of exhibitions in New York City. A more detailed account was presented in the September 11 issue, where it was

stated, without giving a source, that a contract had been
signed a few days prior, the terms of which determined that
the two companies would not run in close opposition to each
other for the next twenty years. And it was agreed that one
of them would be transported to Europe in the spring of 1881
to travel through Great Britain and the continent for the next
five years, and when that show returned the other would be
sent abroad; but, before departure in the spring, both companies would perform in conjunction for a week in New York
City, similar to what the Great London and Forepaugh shows
had done in Philadelphia during April last.[1]

A later announcement, the source being Charles
Brothwell (one of Barnum's "busy bees"), revealed that contracts were completed on September 28 for conveying the
Great London to England under P. T. Barnum's management. Frank Hyatt was to leave the city on the steamship
Canada on October 6 to prepare the way and was to be followed by other agents at intervals throughout the winter.
The show was to begin its exhibit in Liverpool in April of
1881. Further, there was said to be contracts for the transportation of sixty first-class passengers, twenty second class
in charge of the stock, ten elephants, including the baby, ten
camels, eighty horses, fifteen ponies, and six tableau cars.[2]

A confirmation of these developments came with the
announcement of an auction of valuable circus property belonging to Cooper, Bailey & Co. at their winter quarters, 23rd
Street and Columbia Avenue, in Philadelphia. The advertisement included, "The firm having dissolved partnership
and new arrangements having been made contemplating a
TOUR IN EUROPE, all surplus properties will be sold at
auction, as per list below."[3]

The auction took place on November 5, 1880. The
items for sale comprised seventy head of horses and as many
harnesses, ten baggage wagons, five animal cages, several

tents, seats, jacks and stringers, tent poles, pads, wardrobe, newspaper cuts, etc. The principal buyers were Adam Fore-paugh, John O'Brien, and a sideshow man by the name of James McCrystal. Most everything brought low prices and some of the horses were bid so low they were withdrawn by auctioneers Doyle and Nichols.[4]

A few weeks later an advertisement for an auction in New York City clarified the Barnum and Bailey relationship by linking the two shows as one. The text read in part:

> Notice to showmen. An extraordinary enterprise inaugurated. The proprietors of P. T. Barnum's Greatest Show on Earth, the Great London Circus, Sanger's Royal British Menagerie, and the International Grand Allied Shows, positively the largest and very best on the face of the earth, proprietors P. T. Barnum, James A. Bailey and James L. Hutchinson, having perfected a monster consolidation of these two undisputed master shows of the universe, completed the erection and permanent establishing of a grand depot of supplies for showmen, where everything necessary can be obtained for the fitting-out of all classes of tent exhibitions.

The ad indicated this was the inauguration of an annual series of sales and that a permanent "Depot of Supplies Headquarters" was established at Bridgeport, Connecticut, where a new building had been erected.[5]

The first of the advertised auctions took place at the American Institute on December 16. It began around 10:30 a.m. and continued for the better part of the day. Barnum was too ill to attend but his partners, Bailey and James L. Hutchinson represented the company. On the block were tents, wagons, seats, band uniforms, ring costumes, stuffed animals, cages and cage covers, ropes, etc. The sale brought in about $30,000. The live animals had been disposed of in a private sale the previous day for about $20,000, and twenty-two railway cars had also been sold to the John Robinson organization of Cincinnati for $12,000.[6]

These men had great plans of running two shows simultaneously—one abroad and one at home. Barnum had wanted for some years to place a show in Europe under the magic of his name. Earlier he had toyed with taking his Great Roman Hippodrome there, but its second year failure and W. C. Coup's leaving the concern aborted that scheme.

In the end, this great plan never took root. The partners went out with one large show under a combination title for the 1881 tenting season with the advertising stipulating, "United for this season only, and now inaugurating an experimental tour of the whole country at the daily expense of $4,500." An interview with Bailey in his room at the Grand Central Hotel in New York City by a man from the New Haven *Sunday Union* explains the reasoning for the change.

The *Sunday Union* man began with the suggestion: "It is the opinion of many managers that you have a white elephant on your hands—in other words, your new company is too large to travel."

"Yes," Bailey replied, "the consolidation was effected with the idea of taking one half to Europe, but various obstacles arose, the most prominent of which was Mr. Barnum's illness. The matter of running the whole show in the United States was discussed for weeks. But as most of our contracts with artists had already been made it was determined to give the U. S. a show designed for two continents. It will be for this season only."[7]

The enormous task of accomplishing this fell on the slender shoulders of James A. Bailey. It is interesting to note that his hotel room was cluttered with samples of folding chairs, a miniature Roman chariot, an improved electric chandelier, models of cars and cages, lithos of various elephants, a model of a sectional center pole, woodcuts of people and animals, a *papier-mâché* plan of three rings, a tubular boiler and engine, double action ticket boxes, samples of elephant shackles, cordage, books, banners, balloons, Chinese lanterns, ring carpeting, trapeze trappings, etc. Signs of a mind that never rested.

"Is it true that you will give 3 shows daily?" the reporter asked.

"Yes, in all cities of medium size and often in larger ones. We find that families attend morning exhibitions to avoid crowds. Besides, public schools are getting woke up to the advantage afforded by these large menageries. We are in daily receipt of letters from school officials all over the U. S. seeking information. Our great menagerie this season will afford a more comprehensive study of the animal kingdom than any other collection in the world except London's Zoological Garden and the *Jardin d'Aclimation* in Paris."

"How about the electric lights?"

"Well this wonderful discovery has never been shown at its best in this country. We propose to make the electric light a feature and for the first time in history show it for what it is. Our system involves no less than 21 chandeliers, and our entire canvas city, interior and exterior, will be as bright as noon day. The engine and apparatus will be located where all will be able to see—rich or poor, patrons and non-patrons. We will do for the electric light what its discoverer has long sought of individuals and corporations, that is, run it for its practical value."

"Mr. Bailey, there is a rumor that you will spare the public the infliction of wax figures, stuffed snakes and birds, and cheap panoramic views that go to make up the average travelling museum."

"Gone, thank heavens, all gone—sold at auction. Our procession will show 100 vehicles. Every one will contain wild animals or other valuable property. We have about 90 cars and 300 draught horses, but we have no room to drag this trash around the country. In the matter of canvas, I can only say our spread is the largest I have ever seen. The three rings are a necessity—our performers were engaged for two continents and the three rings must be occupied continually to get them all before the public. Our show for 1881 will be known in the amusement records of America as the greatest artistic success of the times."[8]

What was the needfulness for the merging of these two great circuses? An aging Barnum was desirous of perpetuating his name; yet, unlike rival Forepaugh, he had no son to carry it on. The five year lease by the "Flatfoots," the three men who were using that name, was running out in 1880. Although they did not appear ready to retire, Barnum was anxious to put his interests into the hands of younger management. And fortuitously, a bright and energetic entrepreneur named James A. Bailey was proving his genius as an advertiser; and in so doing was giving the Barnum show a whipping with the recently acquired Howes' Great London, which coupled with the Cooper & Bailey outfit created a double show of strong appeal. Then there was the circus of Adam Forepaugh which had become a formidable competitor and an irritant to both circuses.

With Cooper's retirement Bailey was at last solely in charge of a great circus. Why would he, now the owner of a flourishing establishment and in full control of his destiny, want to enter into a business relationship with Barnum? The most satisfying answer can be found in George Middleton's memoirs. The reader may recall that Middleton and Bailey were long time business associates. Bailey told him, Middleton stated, that "if he ever got hold of Barnum's name there would never be a tent made large enough to hold the people."[9] One can be assured that Bailey was observant of the Barnum show from its outset and throughout its full history, and was confident that through his proficiency as an advertiser he could exceed previous successes with the well proven Barnam name, and was lustful for the opportunity to place his own showmanship skills on a level with Barnum's, side by side on a masthead. He saw this as an opportunity and a challenge to ascend to another level.

Yet according to Tody Hamilton, when they became partners, Bailey said to Barnum, "Mr. Barnum, I don't care for your name; I want your capital. My name as a circus man stands above yours; but I need more money, and you've got it. That is the only reason I am entering into this partnership."[10] This sounds a bit absurd, but there is some truth to it. Bailey did not have the financial means to boost his Great International to match his ambitions. The sickly and aging Barnum, at seventy years of age, appeared to be but a partner of short life and minor inconvenience. But once in control of the Barnum name and image, Bailey could daub it on barns and walls from Maine to Oregon *ad infinitum*. A wedding, requiring P. T. Barnum to share his identity on circus advertising with others for the first time, was the result.

FOOTNOTES

PROLOGUE: MR. BARNUM AND MR. BAILEY

[1] Advertisement, Buffalo (NY) *Commercial Advertiser*, August 11, 1848, n.p.n.

[2] Thayer, "Bad Press, Big Crowds," p. 32.

[3] Advertisement, Pittsburgh (PA) *Daily Union*, October 19, 1855, n.p.n.

[4] Barnum, *Struggles and Triumphs*, p. 638.

[5] Comment by W. C. Coup, New York *Clipper*, May 16, 1891, p. 169.

[6] Clipping, "An Old Showman," Atlanta (GA) *Constitution*, February 23, 1891, n.p.n. John Dingess relates the same account in his unpublished manuscript, differing only that the game was chess and Emerson was a clergyman.

[7] Barnum, *Selected Letters*, p. 165.

[8] New York *Clipper*, May 16, 1891, p. 169.

[9] Interview of P. T. Barnum, clipping, *The Era*, July 29, 1877, n.p.n.

[10] Undated newspaper clipping, scrapbook SBK 17, Circus World Museum.

[11] *Ibid.*

[12] Dingess, p. 368.

[13] Clipping, Circus World Museum, "Monarch of Humbug," n.d., n.p.n. It is regrettable that the source of such a controversial account is not more identifiable.

[14] Cooke, "Reminiscences of a Showman," n.p.n.

[15] *Ibid.*

[16] Clipping, M. R. Werner, "The Triumphs of a Super-showman," Chattanooga (TN) *Sunday Times*, September 16, 1923, n.p.n.

[17] Clipping of interview with James E. Cooper, Philadelphia (PA) *Press*, n.d. but probably 1891, n.p.n.

[18] Clipping, New York *Times*, September 19, 1891, n.p.n.

[19] *Ibid.*

[20] *Ibid.*

[21] *Ibid.*

[22] *Ibid*

[23] Clipping, Boston (MA) *Herald*, April 20, 1906, n. p. n.

[24] Clipping, "A Caesar Among showmen," New York *Times*, September 19, 1891, n.p.n.

PART I: P. T. BARNUM'S GREAT BEGINNING

[1] Clipping, "An Old Showman," Atlanta (GA) *Constitution*, February 23, 1891, n.p.n.

[2] Syracuse (NY) *Standard, op. cit.*, n.p.n. The New York *Clipper* listed twenty-six shows that started on the road in 1871: P. T. Barnum's, Van Amburgh & Co. (two units), G. G. Grady's, G. F. Bailey's, Wootten & Haight, C. Y. Noyes'; Rosston, Springer & Henderson; James Robinson's, Cole & Orton, John Robinson's, Agnes Lake's, Adam Forepaugh's, Kincade's, John O'Brien's (three shows), the Commonwealth, P. A. Older's, J. A. Warner & Co., John Stowe & Sons, Alex Robinson's, E. Stowe's, Stone & Murray, Howes London, and L. B. Lent's.

[3] Copy of a Barnum letter to Nathans, Bailey & Co. in the Pfening Collection.

[4] Thayer, "Joseph E. Warner," p. 20.

[5] Newark (NJ) *Daily Advertiser*, April 27, 1871, p. 2.

[6] Albany (NY) *Argus*, August 9, 1871, p. 4.

[7] Quote from the Brooklyn (NY) *Eagle* in the Newark (NJ) *Daily Advertiser*, April 27, 1871, p. 2.

[8] New York *Clipper*, April 22, 1871, p. 23.

[9] Crosby, "The Early Days of Barnum's 'Greatest on Earth'," p. 49.

[10] Newark (NJ) *Daily Advertiser*, April 29, 1871, p. 2.

[11] Garvie, "Old-Time Show Receipts," p. 185.

[12] New York *Clipper*, August 19, 1871, p. 159.

[13] Albany (NY) *Argus*, August 23, 1871, p. 4. Barnum's second day was a repeat of the first. Afternoon crowds were turned away for lack of seating. People from Coxsackie and adjoining

towns came in on a chartered steamer; and others came from
the surrounding countryside by wagon and train.

[14] Utica (NY) *Daily Observer*, September 1, 1871, p. 3.

[15] Andrew Hallidie's electric cable car wasn't invented until 1869.
It was introduced in 1873 in San Francisco, but it took several
more years before it was in universal use.

[16] Richmond (VA) *Daily Dispatch*, June 13, 1855, n.p.n.

[17] Albany (NY) *Argus*, August 9, 1871, p. 4.

[18] New York *Clipper*, August 19, 1871, p. 159.

[19] Re-printed in the New York *Clipper*, May 31, 1871, p. 71, from
the Boston (MA) *Herald* and *Times* of May 18, 1871.

[20] Atlanta (GA) *Constitution*, February 23, 1891, n.p.n.

[21] C. C. Sturtevant article, a clipping in the Chindahl papers. Ma-
jor circuses for 1872: Adam Forepaugh's, Backenstoe's, C. W.
Noyes', Central Park Menagerie, Chiarini's, Commonwealth,
Dan Rice's, G. G. Grady's, George F. Bailey's, Great Eastern,
J. E. Warner & Co., James E. Cooper's, James Robinson's,
James T. Johnson's, John O'Brien's, John Robinson's, Klicker
& Kelly, L. B. Lent's, North American, P. A. Older's, P. T.
Barnum's, Romelli & Co., Rosston, Spring & Henderson, S. Q.
Stokes', Sells Bros.', Smith & Baird, Van Amburgh & Co., W.
W. Cole's.

[22] Barnum, *Struggles and Triumphs*, p. 683.

[23] Coup, p. 65.

[24] *Ibid.*, p. 61.

[25] *Ibid.*, p. 65.

[26] Dahlinger, Part Three, p. 28. He credits newspaper account from
the Lowell (MA) *Weekly Journal*, June 13, 1873.

[27] Coup, *op. cit.*, p. 62.

[28] Email to the author from Stuart Thayer, September 19, 1998.

[29] Cleveland (OH) *Plain Dealer*, June 18, 1872, p. 3.

[30] Evansville (IN) *Daily Journal*, August 3, 1872, p. 4. Luke
Tilden was assistant manager; S. H. Hurd, treasurer and superintendent; W. C. Crum, general agent; W. H. Pease, press
agent; and C. C. Pell, contracting agent; Fritz Hartman, director
of the band.

[31] Barnum, *Struggles and Triumphs*, p. 683.

[32] Evansville (IN) *Daily Journal*, August 3, 1872, p. 4.

[33] Other additions included Mons. de LaRue (this may have been William LaRue, Sr.), bareback rider; Lazelle and Millson, performers on a single trapeze; Signor Jose Monteverde, contortionist; and several subordinate figures as tumblers, leapers, acrobats, and riders. Returning from 1871 were the Marion Sisters, Mlle. Celeste Maria Girardeau (or Fauliere), and Mlle. Carlotta DaVinci. The clowns were Dan Castello and George Madden. Castello also worked his highly-trained horses, Czar, Senator and Flying Cloud. Charles White held forth in the lion cage.

[34] Cleveland (OH) *Plain Dealer*, June 18, 1872, p. 3.

[35] Original copies in the Albert Conover collection, Circus World Museum, Baraboo, WI.

[36] Letter to the author dated October 2, 1999. MacDougall was engineer for the Ringling Bros. and Barnum & Bailey Circus for several years. He estimated the pole to be: two 36' center poles, sixteen 27' long quarter poles, sixteen 22' short quarter poles, and 13' side poles.

[37] Dingess manuscript.

[38] Toledo (OH) *Blade*, June 29, 1872, n.p.n.

[39] Baltimore (MD) *American and Commercial Advertiser*, May 4, 1872, p. 4.

[40] Cleveland (OH) *Plain Dealer*, June 18, 1872, p. 3.

[41] Cincinnati (OH) *Daily Gazette*, July 18, 1872, p. 4.

[42] Chicago (IL) *Inter-Ocean*, October 10, 1872, p. 6.

[43] Cincinnati (OH) *Daily Gazette*, July 18, 1872, p. 4.

[44] Detroit (MI) *Free Press*, October 30, 1872, p. 1.

[45] Another source stated that the idea was Coup's. He and Older were old friends, having worked together on the Yankee Robinson show when Older was the manager.

[46] A partial route included Memphis, Tennessee, November 20, 21; Grenada, Mississippi, 22; Water Valley, 23; Holly Springs, 25; Jackson, Tennessee, 26; Corinth, Mississippi, 27; Tuscumbia, Alabama, 28; Huntsville, 29; Chattanooga, Tennessee, 30; Rome, Georgia, December 2; Dalton, 3; Cartersville, 4; Marietta, 5; and Atlanta, 6.

[47] Taken from the Richard E. Conover notes citing a Coup interview carried in the Baltimore (MD) *Gazette*, n.d., n.p.n.; New York *Clipper*, December 28, 1872, p. 310; Sturtevant, "P. T. Barnum of Connecticut," n.p.n.

[48] Richard E. Conover notes. Conover obtained the terms of Older's purchase from a photostatic copy of the contract in the possession of Tom Parkinson.

[49] Dingess manuscript, pp. 259-260.

[50] Saxon, *P. T. Barnum, the Legend and the Man*, p. 244.

[51] Thayer, *Grand Entrée*, p. 48.

[52] Luke Tilden was assistant manager; Fritz Hartman, band leader; W. L. Jukes, museum manager; Charles White, menagerie manager; Dr. Asa Berry, veterinarian; Peter Halstead, master of transportation; George Coup, candy privilege.

[53] Buffalo (NY) *Daily Courier*, July 2, 1873, p. 2.

[54] Baltimore (MD) *American and Commercial Advertiser*, September 23, 1873, p. 4.

[55] Pittsburgh (PA) *Post*, July 9, 1873, p. 4.

[56] Baltimore (MD) *American and Commercial Advertiser*, September 23, 1873, p. 4.

[57] Titusville (PA) *Morning Herald*, July 7, 1873.

[58] Buffalo (NY) *Daily Courier*, July 2, 1873, p. 2.

[59] *Ibid.*

[60] Boston (MA) *Globe*, May 21, 1873, p. 8.

[61] Syracuse (NY) *Standard*, circa 1899, n.p.n.

[62] *Frank Leslie's Illustrated Weekly*, April 5, 1873, p. 66.

[63] Buffalo (NY) *Daily Courier*, July 2, 1873, p. 2.

[64] Cleveland (OH) *Plain Dealer*, July 15, 1873, p. 3.

[65] Pittsburgh (PA) *Post*, July 4, 1873, p. 1.

[66] New York *Clipper*, September 27, 1873, p. 207.

[67] Fritz Hartman's orchestra provided an overture, followed by the Grand Hippodrome Entree, a spectacle called "The Halt in the Desert," this being the fourth straight season that Coup and Castello had begun a program with this theme. Dan Bushnell and wife juggled on the slack-wire and presented an impalement act in which Mrs. Bushnell was the target for knives and axes thrown by her husband. There was the Mathews Family

of acrobats, including Arthur Gregory and Theodore Mathews
on the horizontal bars. Signor Sebastian, one of the finest of
living equestrians, rode bareback, and did a carrying act with
his infant son, Louis; another son, Romeo, was a pad rider.
Master Dave Castello performed a somersault equestrian act
without saddle or bridle. Arthur Nelson and wife were scenic
riders. Lazelle & Millson performed on the trapeze. Dan Castello put his trick horse through its paces. Mons. D'Atalie and
wife performed feats of strength and an iron jaw act. James
Messenger caught cannon balls. Both Lucille Watson and Vin-
nie Cooke rode principal acts. There was also the equestrian
goat, Alexis; the performing elephants, Gypsy and Betsy, Jerry
Hopper's stilt act, George North's scenic riding, Frank Barry's
bareback riding, and Sergeant Burke's Zouave-drill act. Clown
alley was occupied by Gus Lee, Walter Aymar, Jerry Hopper,
and George and Jerry Mathews. Add to this the famous midget
Commodore Nutt who, for the first time, appear in the role of
clown. Frank Whittaker was the equestrian director and Horace
Nichols, the ringmaster. Signor Sebastian, Lucille Watson and
Frank Barry were all true stars of the ring. The Mathews Family, eight acrobats, were newly arrived from England, where
their work had been well received. The D'Atalies were a top
strength act from France. The Castellos, the Bushnells, George
North, and Lazelle & Millson were repeating their 1872 appearances on the program. James Melville, the leading rider in
the previous season, was gone, and his absence was the greatest
difference between the 1872 and 1873 seasons.

[68] Buffalo (NY) *Daily Courier*, July 2, 1873, p. 2.

[69] Titusville (PA) *Morning Herald*, July 7, 1873.

[70] In the Bunnell sideshow, a separate operation, were Colonel
Goshen, the "Arabian" giant, who was seven feet eleven inches
tall, and 620 pounds in weight; Isaac Sprague, a living skeleton; Mme. Clark, a fat lady; two albino ladies, Ella Mann and
Etta Rogers; and Maximo and Bartola, the famous Aztec children.

[71] Barnum, "Selected Letters," pp. 126-127.

[72] In 1876 the W. W. Cole circus used a cannon on the train to announce the arrival into town. The cannon shot was also repeated to signal the start of the parade.

[73] Boston (MA) *Daily Courier*, July 1, 1873, p. 2.

[74] Buffalo (NY) *Daily Courier*, July 2, 1873, p. 2.

[75] *Frank Leslie's Illustrated Weekly*, April 5, 1873, p. 66.

[76] Pittsburgh (PA) *Post*, July 9, 1873, p. 4.

[77] Battle Creek (MI) *Daily Journal*, July 18, 1873, p. 4.

[78] Jackson (MI) *Daily Citizen*, August 23, 1873, quoting the Troy (NY) *Budget*.

[79] 1873 Barnum route book, pp. 31-32.

[80] Rochester (NY) *Evening Express*, June 28, 1873, p. 2.

[81] New York *Clipper*, November 1, 1873, p. 246.

[82] New York *Times*, November 21, 1873, p. 4.

[83] *Ibid.*

[84] Buffalo (NY) *Daily Courier*, July 3, 1873, p. 2.

PART II: THE SAGA OF HOWES' GREAT LONDON

[1] Major shows on the road were Adam Forepaugh's, the Empire City, Hemmings & Cooper, Col. C. T. Ames', Yankee Robinson's, John Robinson's, Great European, Stone & Murray, P. T. Barnum's, L. B. Lent's, Van Amburgh's (menagerie only), Rosston-Stringer-Henderson, James Robinson's, P. A. Older's, J. A. Wallace's, Lakes Hippo-Olympiad, W. W. Cole's, Backenstroe's, C. W. Noyes'.

[2] Thayer, *Annals*, Vol. I, p. 174.

[3] A partial route was revealed in the foreign entertainment news of the New York *Clipper*. Preston, June 15; Dewsbury, 20; Barnsley, 25; Melton Mowbray, July 6; Cambridge, 21-22; Norwich, August 1-2; Edmunds, 8; Ipswich, 11; Rochester, 27; Portsmouth, September 19-20; Taunton, October 11; Bristol, 17. There was also an item in the *Clipper* of July 2 that read: "Howes and Cushings Circus is at present located in the Knott Mill Fair Ground, Manchester, and attracts numerous visitors. A grand procession through the town takes place daily and is a handsome spectacle."

[4] Sturtevant, "Little Biographies," No. 7, p. 3.

[5] Frost, pp. 191-192.

[6] The managerial assistants: Capt. Thomas Christopher, treasurer; Green Berry, general agent; John Tryon, press agent; C. Richardson, master of canvas; William Lewis, master of horse; Roberts, costumer; George White, keeper of chariots; Edward Gray, keeper of carriages and vans. The music was supplied by Emidy's British Cornet Band. J. H. Charmou served as master of the ring.

[7] Rochester (NY) *Evening Express*, July 7, 1871, p. 2. In 1892, with Wombwell's Menagerie, Hednesford, Staffordshire, England, Delhi Montano was torn to pieces while performing in a cage of three bears and a hyena.

[8] New York *Times*, July 23, 1871, p. 5.

[9] New York *Times*, July 24, 1871, p. 3.

[10] New York *Clipper*, August 12, 1871, p. 151; letter to Richard J. Reynolds III from Richard W. Flint, dated February 9, 1997, quoting the Brewster (NY) *Standard* of July 29, 1871.

[11] Toronto (Canada) *Daily Telegram*, August 7, 1871, p. 4.

[12] Ontario (Canada) *Reformer*, August 11, 1871, pp. 2, 3.

[13] New York *Clipper*, April 15, 1871, p. 15.

[14] A. Pember, pp. 221-222.

[15] New York *Times*, April 18, 1871, p. 4. The Lockport, NY, date of the July 12 proved unfortunate. The Globe Tableau wagon broke through a bridge four miles from the city. The front wheels and axle were broken and the body slightly damaged, requiring four days of repair work.

[16] Conover, notes.

[17] The administrative corps consisted of Egbert Howes, manager; Green Berry, contracting agent; Elbert Howes, ticket agent; and Capt. T. D. Christopher, treasurer. As for ring performers, there were the versatile Jee family; riders Lilly Meers, W. H. Morgan, John Saunders; clowns Signor Almonte, James Cooke; and gymnasts, E. and T. Faust, W. Ector, Signor Hernandez, Don Leonti, etc. Major circuses on the road for 1882 were Backenstoe's, John Robinson's, C. W. Noyes', Sells Bros.', P. T. Barnum's, G. G. Grady's, Van Amburgh's (menagerie

only), Central Park, Conklin Bros.' Commonwealth, James Robinson's, L. B. Lent's, Dan Rice's, S. Q. Stokes', J. E. Warner's, James E. Cooper's, Smith & Baird's, P. A. Older's, Romelli & Co.

[18] Clipping, St. Louis (MO) *Globe-Democrat*, May 29, 1880, n.p.n.

[19] New York *Clipper*, July 22, 1871, p. 127.

[20] Pittsburgh (PA) *Post*, July 4, 1873, p. 1. In keeping with the course of ill fortune being traveled, a terrific storm hit on opening night of the Pittsburgh stand. An unusually heavy gust of wind struck the main pavilion at about 9:45 p.m. while the show was in progress. Almost immediately the center poles gave way and the tent caved in on the audience. The canvas caught fire from the gas burners around the center poles, but was shortly extinguished by the downpour of rain. Miraculously, no one was killed, no one was seriously injured, and only a few received bruises. One of the elephants wandered off but was soon returned to the show lot. A few cages were blown over with no damage to their frightened residents.

[21] The veteran John Tryon was press agent; C. Clark, contracting agent; James Cooke, equestrian director; and Joseph Emidy, band leader.

[22] Gymnastics were performed by the Romelli Family. The clowns were James Cooke and Joseph Kennebel. Hurdle rider William H. Morgan was the one principal returning from the previous year.

[23] Jackson (MI) *Daily Citizen*, June 5, 1874, p. 4. The 1874 company was very similar to the previous year. Richard H. and Elise Dockrill and Joseph Kennebel were featured attractions, along with the aerialist Romelli troupe—Eugene, Marie, and son Carlos—and their "Iron Cradle" and "Chair Perche" performed fifty feet above the ground. Mlle. Cordelia handled the female bareback riding duties, jumping through hoops in every conceivable shape and manner. The trained animal acts—the five-elephant pyramid, five man-eating hyenas, and five royal Bengal tigers—continued to astound. The addition of the Central Park Menagerie expanded the animal exhibits to fifty cages

and along with them came a band of Iroquois Indians. There
were, however, new administrative faces for this season. Egbert Howes and Capt. Thomas Christopher sold their part ownership to Kelley. John Lyke replaced Christopher as treasurer.
Green Berry was back after missing 1873, this time as contracting agent. T. R. Toole was the press agent. Den Stone was
in charge of the arena production. Homer Davis had the privileges.

24 Reprinted in the Kansas City (MO) *Journal of Commerce*, May
    30, 1875, p. 4.
25 Advertisement for Fond du Lac (WI) newspaper, announcing
    the performance date for August 12. The performances were
    led by the riding of Fred Barclay and Charles Reed; and Fred
    O'Brien threw somersaults over five elephants and double
    somersaults over three of them. The versatile Lee family was
    there—H. C., Harry, Lavater, Rosa and little Robert. The
    equestienne feats were performed by Jeannette Watson and
    Mlle. Cordelia; William Conrad presented his dog act; Prof.
    Johnson handled the tigers. And let us not neglect the addition
    of an Iroquois Indian troupe. George Middleton and W. H.
    Gardner owned the privileges.
26 Reprinted in the Kansas City (MO) *Journal of Commerce*, May
    30, 1875, p. 4.
27 Kansas City (MO) *Journal of Commerce*, June 1, 1875, p. 4.
28 St. Joseph (MO) *Daily Morning Herald*, June 2, 1875, p. 4.
29 St. Joseph (MO) *Daily Morning Herald*, June 4, 1875, p. 4.
30 New York *Clipper*, July 24, 1875, p. 134.
31 E-mail to the author, May 9, 1998.
32 While in Memphis, Tennessee, for a September 13 and 14 stand,
    the sideshow was attached by the sheriff to satisfy a claim of
    $17,000 by unidentified parties in New York.
33 Clipping, Chicago (ILO) *Inter Ocean*, September 5, 1876, n.p.n.
34 Chicago (IL) *Daily Tribune*, June 22, 1876, p. 8. Others in-
    cluded Mme. Elise Dockrill, four-horse rider; Mlle. Emma Ju-
    tau, trapezist; R. H. Dockrill, *manège* act with his trained horse
    Ellington; Howard Dorr and pupils, gymnasts; Henry Dorr,
    triple horizontal bar; George Brown, trapezist; William Con-

well, contortionist; Fred O'Brien, champion leaper; and clowns Ben Maginley and William Conrad. The ringmaster was Robert Ellingham.

[35] Evansville (IN) *Daily Journal*, June 7, 1876, p. 8. The principal performers for 1876 were led by the daring equestrian James Melville. He was accompanied by his son Frank, a graceful and accomplished rider in his own right, and little Alexander, described as "phenomenally interesting and cunning." William Batcheller and William Worland were standouts over a group of leapers who turned somersaults over a number of elephants. There was also the "mechanic's act" in which city boys were taught to ride in a circus by means of a derrick-like "Stokes mechanic" device.

[36] Clipping, Chicago (IL) *Inter Ocean*, September 5, 1876, n.p.n.

[37] New York *Mercury*, April 29, 1876, n.p.n.

[38] Augusta (GA) *Chronicle and Sentinel*, January 17, 1877, p. 4.

[39] The car rental company had an attachment served on the show while it was in Savannah, Georgia, but it was withdrawn when the circus management paid $1,000 on the claim and promised to pay the balance as soon money came in.

[40] The show property, as listed in the Augusta (GA) *Chronicle and Sentinel* of January 18, 1877, consisted of the following: 100 work and ring horses, 29 ponies, 5 elephants, 5 Royal Bengal tigers, 8 hyenas, 2 lionesses, 3 cubs, 1 lion, 1 jaguar, 5 panthers, 1 yak, 1 eland, 2 peccaries, 1 hartebeest, 1 partaquare, 2 antelopes, 1 llama, 1 sacred cow, 1 elk, 1 zebra, 1 camel, 1 emu, 16 cages for animals, 3 cages of birds and small animals, 2 tableaux cars, 2 railroad cars, 1 bandwagon, 1 glass wagon, 1 small chaise, 1 dragon chariot, 1 ticket wagon, 6 truck wagons, 2 stringer wagons, 1 pole wagon, 4 London wagons, 2 three-center-pole circus tents, 1 two-center-pole menagerie tent, 1 dressing room tent, 4 horse tents, 2 cook tents, 8 lengths of reserved seats, 30 lengths of plain seats, plus all of the bedding and other miscellaneous items.

[41] Augusta (GA) *Chronicle and Sentinel*, January 30, 1877, p. 4.

[42] Augusta (GA) *Chronicle and Sentinel*, February 2, 1877, p. 4.

[43] Augusta (GA) *Chronicle and Sentinal*, January 18, 1877, p. 4;
Februrary 3 and 4, 1877, pp. 4.

[44] Augusta (GA) *Chronicle and Sentinel*, April 10, 1877, p. 4.

[45] *Ibid.* We can get an idea of the usual performance roster from a
description by a Boston correspondent for the *Clipper*. The
grand entree was followed by Carrie Boshell's slack-wire act;
R. H. Dockrill's *manège* act; Livingston Brothers and the Victorelli Brothers performing on the horizontal bars, with William Conrad as clown; somersault bareback by Frank Melville,
clowned by Johnny Patterson; battoute leaps by the company;
Fred O'Brien in a double somersault over five elephants; principal act by Mme. Dockrill, clowned by William Conrad; a
brother act by the Victorellis; bounding jockey by Frank Melville, clowned by Charley McCarthy; five performing elephant
handled by George Arstingstall; tumbling by the company;
four-horse act by Mme. Dockrill; the Lawrence Sisters on the
trapeze; the Victorellis as comical musical clowns; and finishing with a den of performing tigers. Not included in the *Clipper*
account were other members of the O'Brien family. Mme.
O'Brien worked the slack-wire and sons Willie and Freddie did
a trapeze act.

[46] *Ibid.*

[47] New York *Clipper*, June 16, 1877, p. 94.

[48] Boston (MA) *Herald*, June 5, 1877, reprinted in the New York
Clipper, June 30, 1877, p. 111; Toronto (Canada) *Daily
Leader*, August 18, 1877, reprinted in the New York *Clipper*,
September 8, 1877, p. 191.

[49] New York *Clipper*, August 18, 1877, p. 166.

[50] The circus opened the season at Gilmore's Garden, New York
City, on March 25 with a strong program. (1) The grand entree
and Mardi Gras carnival, headed by James Robinson's band
attired in military dress. (2) French clown Joseph Kennebel, a
burlesque of an entry rider. (3) William Gorman, a hurricane
hurdle act. (4) Acrobatic feats by the company. (5) Pauline Lee,
juggling on horseback to the clowning of Johnny Patterson. (6)
R. H. Dockrill and his *manège* horse Ellington. (7) Joseph
Kennebel, a burlesque of the previous act riding a "basket

horse." (8) Feats of a bareback riding monkey. (9) Acrobatic skills, the Livingston Brothers and John Murtz. (10) Mme. Dockrill, principal and flying hurdle act. (11) Kennebel Brothers, panomime clowning, ending with a burlesque duel with pistols. (12) Five trained elephants worked by George Arstingstall. (13) Mme. Dockrill, four-horse act. (14) Mme. Josephine and W. Hines, double trapeze performance. (15) the great James Robinson, bareback act to the clowning of Johnny Patterson. (16) Ending with Frank Garner leaping over elephants.[50] There were also references to the Miranda Sisters and to the Lenton Brothers. [New York *Clipper*, April 6, 1878, p. 14.]

[51] King, Chapter 2, Part Two, p. 57.
[52] *Ibid*, p, 58.
[53] *Ibid*.
[54] *Ibid*.
[55] *Ibid*.

PART III: THE BARNUM SHOW—AFTER COUP

[1] C. G. Sturtevant, "Little Biographies," February, 1929, p. 4.
[2] George L. Chindahl, p. 103. There are occasionally specific references to O'Brien malpractice. In 1878, for example, Linda Jeal and husband, William O'Dale Stevens, were on O'Brien's Campbell's Circus, but after leaving in late August had to sue to get their horse and wardrobe properties [Draper, "Linda Jeal and Her Equestrian Kin," p. 31].
[3] Hamilton, St. Louis (MO) *Globe Democrat*, April 14, 1907, n.p.n.
[4] *Ibid.*
[5] Clipping, Janesville (WI) *City News*, August 19, 1875, n.p.n.
[6] Hamilton, *op. cit.*, n.p.n.
[7] Clipping, Kenosha (WI) *Telegraph*, September 2, 1875, n.p.n.
[8] Clarke, p. 324.
[9] Conklin, pp. 22-28.
[10] Day, pp. 27-28.
[11] New York *Clipper*, September 3, 1864, p. 167.
[12] Clarke, *op. cit.*, p. 324.
[13] New York *Clipper*, November 13, 1880, p. 272.

[14] Utica (NY) *Daily Observer,* September 17, 1874, p. 3.

[15] Toronto (Canada) *Globe,* August 4, 1874, p. 4. James Cooke showed off Dan Castello's trained horse, Senator, and his comic mules, Pete and Barney. The animals having no place with the Hippodrome, were part of O'Brien's lease, as were the museum wagons and many of the cages and their contents. Jerry Hopper created a high degree of gaiety with his stilt act, "which afforded more amusement to the younger portion of the audience than anything else, the grotesque appearance of a man of ordinary proportions corporeally, but at least twenty feet high, affording them the most unbounded source of fun and merriment." The program was concluded by Mr. And Mrs. Nelson. According to the *Globe,* they "illustrated with great force the national characteristics of England, Ireland, and Scotland, changing their dresses without dismounting, so as to represent the costumes usually associated with the popular idea of the three countries."

[16] *Ibid.*

[17] *Ibid.*

[18] Wilmington (DE) *Every Evening,* April 17, 1874, p. 4.

[19] Clipping, Cleveland (OH) *Herald,* December 22, 1875, n.p.n.

[20] *Ibid.*

[21] 1876 Barnum *Advance Courier,* p. 4.

[22] Conklin, *op. cit.,* p. 31.

[23] New York *Times,* January 21, 1876, p. 8.

[24] Sturtevant, "Little Biographies of Famous American Circus Men," May, 1928, p. 5.

[25] 1876 Barnum *Advance Courier,* p. 4.

[26] New York *Clipper,* December 4, 1875, p. 286.

[27] New York *Clipper,* December 11, 1875, p. 295.

[28] *Billboard,* March 19, 1910, p. 23.

[29] Addison M. Nathans, John J.'s younger brother, was assistant to Bailey. In the entertainment area, Walter Waterman was manager of amusements; Francis M. Whittaker, arenic director; W. L. Jukes, superintendent of automatic and mechanical departments; Charles White, superintendent of zoological gardens; Prof. Joseph Withers, general musical director; J. Russell

Haynes, leader of the centennial chorus; and Señora Donetti, Prima Donna. The advertising corps was headed by Charles Stow as editor and general press agent. Dan B. Hopkins and A. Case were press agents; and Lewis June, advance manager. Fred Couldock and Fred A. Keeler were the contracting agents, and F. A. Bartlett the excursion agent. Barnum's autobiography was still being peddled, with J. Fidler serving as the agent.

[30] Barnum, *Selected Letters of P. T. Barnum*, p. 197.

[31] New York *Times*, April 28, 1876.

[32] Additional performers included and Satsuma and Little Allright, Japanese acrobats. Jerry Hopper and George M. Clark were the principal clowns. The corps of leapers, tumblers, and acrobats was made up of Charles Davis, Tom Watson, Lew Whittaker, William Rolland, Tom Clifford, and John Saunders. Señora Satsuma and Mrs. Clifford were entree riders. There was also a centennial chorus, much of which must have been arranged for locally. The ring program opened with an opulent "Oriental Cavalcade by Mounted Knights," followed by the entree of living curiosities—Admiral Dot, the Circassian girl, the "What Is It?" etc. Following in order, William Rolland rode a principal act; Satsuma and Little All Right performed a Japanese tub act; Amelia Carlo rode a "scarf act"; William Carlo introduced his trick ponies; the three Carlo brothers displayed acrobatic feats while playing violins; Jeanette Watson rode a principal act, leaping over banners and through balloons; Satsuma and Little All Right returned on the Japanese ladder; Martinho Lowande and young Tony rode a principal act ("the little boy displayed much nerve and no little degree of skill"); the Carlo brothers encored with more acrobatic feats; Jerry Hopper created laughter on stilts; Martinho Lowande returned to the ring with his four-horse act; Charles White demonstrated his mastery over his trained elephants; and the whole closed with the singing of national songs by the circus chorus.

[33] Various newspaper advertisements, 1876, 1877.

[34] P. T. Barnum *Advance Courier*, 1876, p. 15. The following authors were listed: O. W. Holmes, R. M. Hodges, Samuel A. Green, Joseph S. Jones, S. J. McDougall.

[35] This was comprised of Charles and Carrie Austin in their Challenge Musket Drill; Prof. Charles Young, ventriloquist; Dick Sands, clog dancer; Dan Luke, Ethiopian comedian; Holbrooke & Hughes, a song and dance team; Miss Marion Young, serio-comique; and two more comedians, Charles T. Ellis and Tom St. Clair. Adding to the centennial celebration was a pyrotechnic display following each evening performance. This was under the supervision of Ed F. Linton, with the fireworks manufactured by The Unexcelled Fireworks Company, 112 Chambers Street, New York City. At Elmira, New York, on the afternoon of September 13, tragedy struck during the "Star Spangled Banner" spectacle. Thomas Lee, the gunner in charge of firing the cannon, had his left arm shattered when the piece fired prematurely. The extent of the injury required amputation of the arm. The management paid his salary in full, his hotel and doctor bills, and left someone to care for him until he fully recovered. Members of the company took up a collection for him that amounted to $500.

[36] *Billboard*, March 19, 1910, p. 23.

[37] Hartford (CT) *Daily Courant*, May 18, 1876, p. 2.

[38] *Ibid.*

[39] Clipping, St. John (New Brunswick) *Telegraph*, July 28, 1876, n.p.n.

[40] *Ibid.*

[41] Copy of undated letter in the Pfening Collection.

[42] Clipping, Chicago (IL) *Inter-Ocean*, September 5, 1876, n.p.n.

[43] The principal circuses that toured in 1876 were Barnum's; Cooper & Bailey; Adam Forepaugh; Cooke's; Great European; Hilliard, Hamilton & Hunting's; L. B. Lent's; Montgomery Queen's; Burr Robbins'; John Robinson's; Stickney's; Van Amburgh's; J. E. Warner's.

[44] Clipping, Cleveland (OH) *Herald*, July 15, 1878, n.p.n.

[45] The executive breakdown listed in the 1877 route book included P. T. Barnum, proprietor; George F. Bailey, general manager; A. M. Nathans, assistant manager; Lewis June, general agent; Charles Stow (in advance by two or three weeks) and Fred Lawrence (traveling with the show), press agents; Benjamin

Fish, treasurer; J. J. Nathans, general purchasing agent; Walter Waterman, contracting agent. Charles McLean was superintendent of pavilions; W. L. Jukes, superintendent of the museum; Felix MacDonald, superintendent of the menagerie; Ben Maginley, equestrian director; Frank Howes, ringmaster.

[46] Leading the way was a chariot pulled by fourteen horses and carrying Prof. Wilber's New York Band. This was followed by a number of cages and museum wagons, including an open den of four performing lions, and all decorated with ornaments of mythological and historical figures. Then came the Chariot of Liberty, carrying a replica of the famous bell, allegedly resembling in weight, size and general appearance that of the original that hung in Independence Hall. The great peals coming from it were heard above the reverberating sounds emitted from the other musical units in the procession. This unique chariot was drawn by the four Barnum elephants. Directly behind were a troop of camels. Then came more cages, decorated with scenes from the American landscape, reflecting its lakes, rivers, and mountains. Behind was a cage with glass sides, allowing one to behold a snake charmer within, surrounded by various serpents and enrapt by a huge anaconda. Then more museum wagons, some with automatons in full movement on the roof. Next, a gold encrusted Atlantean chariot with the "Goddess of Liberty" seated atop, surrounded by damsels representing the various nations. Queen Mab's fairy couch followed, pulled by a score of Shetland ponies. Then a car with massive chime bells, playing such melodies as "Hold the Fort," "Ninety and Nine," and other patriotic favorites. And finally there was the calliope, or "steam piano." For a local description we defer to a witness thereof: "This ponderous and unique instrument is placed upon a platform, and in its rear is a beautiful silvered stationary engine; the engineer in charge is seen generating steam, and in front of the engine sits a graceful and accomplished young lady who presides at this steam piano." [Clipping, Bloomington (IL) *Pantagraph*, August 11, 1877, n.p.n.] An 1877 *P. T. Barnum's Daily Show Programme* listed seventeen arenic acts. The entertainment started with the traditional

grand entree, the entire company participating, together with
elephants, camels, ponies, mules, etc. Bringing up the rear was
the parade of curiosities, which included Admiral Dot and
Capt. Costentenus, the Greek tattooed man. The ring performance opened with a principal somersault act by Charles Reed,
supported by Ben Maginley as clown. Then there were the
gymnastics of the Miaco Brothers. Scenic riding, "The Red
Man of the Prairie and his Pony," of Dave Castello. Millie De
Granville's feats of strength and iron jaw demonstration, who
was described by the Janesville, Wisconsin, *City Times* as a fe-
rocious looking female with blond hair. The riding of William
Aymar. Satsuma and All Right's Japanese feats. Tumbling by
the company. Cavorting of comic mules. Jennie Watson's principal equestrienne act. Gymnastics again by the Leotard Brothers. Two stallions ridden and driven in tandem by England's
"side-saddle queen," Jennie Louise Hengler, elegantly aristo-
cratic. A Satsuma encore. Principal bareback riding by the
featured equestrian, Charles Fish. Barnum's stud of six performing Trakene stallions were introduced by Mons. Oscar.
The program concluded with trained elephants handled by
Felix McDonald.

[47] Clipping, Chicago (IL) *Inter-Ocean*, August 12, 1879, n.p.n.

[48] Clipping, Janesville (WI) *The City Times*, June 10, 1880; July
19, 1877, n.p.n.

[49] For this additional price one could observe Miss Annie Wood,
"The Mormon Giant Girl"; the German Midgets, a brother and
two sisters, performing a Lilliputian concert; Walter Stuart,
born without arms and legs but able to write, feed himself,
shave, "a living illustration of what a head and body can do";
the Madagascar Family, mother, father, and son, "highly interesting, musical, and peculiar people"; Zoe Melike, "the only
genuine" Circassian Lady; the Leopard Boy, spotted from head
to foot; and Hiawanata, the Australian Bushman. Included was
an extensive variety show, consisting of a magician, Herr
Schlam, the German Wizard; character sketches by John W.
Whiston, "man of many faces"; Bernard McCreddie, a Scotch
musician who produced melodies with brooms, cigar boxes,

cuspadores, corks, pipes, crackers, and who knows what;
George Kurtz and Nellie Brooks in German, Irish, serio-comic
and melodramatic sketches; John and Amy Tudor, high pedes-
tal and armor dancers; Joseph Lucasie, Madagascarine violinist; and, not the least, Dick Sands, clog dancer and comic Irish
impersonator. Lecturers for the exhibitions were Prof. William
Hutchings, "the original lightning calculator," and Prof. Al
Winters. The whole exhibition represented a unique combination of sideshow oddities and variety performers.

[50] New York *Clipper*, August 4, 1877, p. 150. One of the high-
lights of the season occurred while the show exhibited at
Washington, DC, on October 26 and 27. During the run Barnum called upon President Hayes and family at the White
House. By special request S. S. Smith and Captain Costentenus visited the place as well, where Costentenus was presented with a gold medal by the President.

[51] Mills, pp. 10-11. The Barnum people killed were Jack Breeze,
foreman; Green Berry, excursion agent; Charles Thompson,
program agent; F. A. Baker, program agent; Andrew Mack,
poster; George Rockwell, poster; John Brosell, poster. Injured
were Henry Jennings, lithographer; William Clayton, poster;
Abner West, poster; Edward Dunn, poster; James Baker,
poster. Uninjured were F. A. Keeler, conductor; A. E. Fling,
program agent.

[52] *Ibid.*

[53] Chicago (IL) *Inter-Ocean*, August 13, 1879, n.p.n.

[54] *P. T. Barnum's Illustrated News*, 1878.

[55] New York *Clipper*, May 18, 1878, p. 63.

[56] New York *Clipper*, May 25, 1878, p.71.

[57] *Ibid.*

[58] New York *Clipper*, June 1, 1878, p. 79.

[59] Clipping, Clinton (IA) *The Clinton Age*, August 31, 1877, n.p.n.

[60] St. Louis (MO) *Post-Dispatch*, August 11, 1879, n.p.n.

[61] Clipping, Chicago (IL) *Inter-Ocean*, August 13, 1879, n.p.n.

[62] Clipping, Chicago (IL) *Inter-Ocean*, August 12, 1879, n.p.n.

[63] *Ibid.*

[64] The continuity of arenic events comes from the 1879 "Programme" for the season's opener, followed in this order: (1) A processional pageant with some manner of an oriental theme. (2) The parade of Living Curiosities—the tattooed Capt. Costentenus; the Palestine Giant, Col. Goshen; and Minnie Keeler, the little Queen Mab. (3) Introduction of the Royal Stallions, Mamaluke and Pasha, by Carl Antony. (4) William O'Dale Stevens' Golden Table and Globe Act. (5) Principal Equestrienne Act by Senora Marcellus, with the clown James Holloway. (6) The Egyptian jugglers' Feats of Magic. (7) Principal Bareback Act by Katie Stokes, with clown Charlie Seeley. (8) The Herbert Brothers in Poses Plastique and Acrobatic Feats. (9) Linda Jeal, "the Great and Only" hurdle rider. (10) The leaping stallion, Malakoff, as trained by Carl Antony. (11) Madame Dockrell "in her Great Flying Sensational Act— The Sprite of the Rainbow." (12) Les Comiques by the Miaco Brothers. (13) Emma Lake's manege act. (14) Six Royal Russian Stallions of Carl Anthony's. (15) Madame Dockrill's four-horse act. (16) "Scenes du Cirque" by the company. (17) Pony act of leaping, balancing, and jumping, under the whip of James Cooke. (18) Dashing bareback act of Signor Sebastian. (19) Antony's coal black Royal Trakene Stallions. (20) Ensemble leaping, featuring John Batcheller's double somersault over six elephants. The parade order, taken from the Buffalo *Courier*, began with the chariot of Prof. Withers' Regimental Band; followed by fifteen performing stallions, the glass snake cage, a cage of 300 monkeys, a drove of camels (including one white and one black), the Neptune Chariot, cages with a rhino, giraffe, and a marine aquarium, eight elephants, ostriches, the steam Melochor drawn by an eight-horse hitch, the pony coach of Queen Mab, a line of museum cars with automated figures, and, finally, a calliope. [Buffalo (NY) *Courier*, July 18, 1879.]

[65] Rochester (NY) Daily Union and Advertiser, May 17, 1875, p. 2.

[66] New York *Clipper*, October 16, 1875, p. 231.

[67] Chicago (IL) *Inter-Ocean*, August 12, 1879, n.p.n.

[68] *Ibid.*

[69] *Ibid.*

[70] New York *Clipper*, July 10, 1875, p. 118.

[71] Chicago (IL) *Inter-Ocean*, August 12, 1879, n.p.n. The reader will notice that the meeting date of "June" conflicts with America's Racing Association collapse in "May."

[72] *Ibid.*

[73] Clipping, Milwaukee (WI) *Sentinel*, June 22, 1880, n.p.n.

[74] Clipping, Janesville (WI) *Daily Recorder*, June 30, 1880, n.p.n.

[75] Clipping, Chicago (IL) *Inter-Ocean*, June 1, 1880, n.p.n.

[76] Clipping, Janesville (WI) *City Times*, June 10, 1880, n.p.n.

[77] Clipping, Janesville (WI) *City Times*, July 8, 1880, n.p.n.

PART IV: EMERGENCE OF COOPER & BAILEY

[1] Conover notes.

[2] *Ibid.*

[3] The remaining roster was comprised of Mlle. Carlotta, Chinese juggling on the trapeze; Mons. Lucas D. and Mme. Olivia Parento, double trapeze; Curt Wells, clown, leaper, tumbler, Negro delineator; Charles A. Parento, horizontal bar, giant swing, imitation of Dutch character; Palmer Brothers, Robert and Harry, flying trapeze and leap for life; Fred Kline, ceiling walker, leaper, tumbler, horizontal bar performer; Miss Alice LaPierre, vocalist and character change artist; Marian Norwood, serio-comic artist; Mattie Spear, serio-comic and sentimental vocalist; Marietta Sisters. C. E. Cooper was ringmaster; F. R. Lemen, band leader. There was a wire ascension each afternoon and evening. George Harding was general agent; Frank M. Forrest, contracting agent. A minstrel show was used for the concert, during which Lucas Parento performed the Indian Box Mystery, an escape act.

[4] King, Chapter 2, Part One, p. 26.

[5] Other performers were Pauline Lee and Kate Holloway, equestriennes; Frances DeCodova, iron-jaw lady; Little Victoria, child gymnast; William E. Gorman, bounding jockey; George Holland, principal act; the Milton Jaspers (Newton, Thomas, Clinton), gymnasts; Luke Rivers, equestrian; Miller Brothers,

horizontal bars; James Cassim & Edward Fritz, specialty gymnasts; Prof. George W. Johnston, elephant trainer and wild beast performer; and Pete Conklin, George Madden, and J. N. Rentfrow, clowns. Sam Rinehart was the ringmaster; Phil Diefenbach started as equestrian director but was succeeded by Pete Conklin; Prof. J. H. Kinslow, the band leader; Arthur G. Palmer, calliope player. Performers added throughout the season include the Siegrist Children (Louis, Thomas, Willie), acrobats; François and his trained dogs; Charles Seeley and Sam Rinehart, clowns and leapers; James Murray, tumbler; and the Belmonts (Charles, Lolino), trapeze artists. The sideshow was orated by Edward J. Sackett. Within the tent were Annie Leak, armless lady; Charlotte Moxley, English giantess; Pearle and Henry Foster, White Haired People of the Isle; Prof. H. Everett, Punch and Judy and magician; plus performing monkeys, cosmoramic views, and snakes.

[6] King, Chapter 2, Part One, p. 29.

[7] New York *Clipper*, November 18, 1876, p. 271. The sale netted around $20,000. Sixty-five draught horses were sold for over $100 each; two mares, $310 and $180 each; and pairs at $480, $350, and $325; six Shetland ponies, with $70 being the most for any one of the lot; ten mules, totaled $1,800; the Sacred Cow and Calf, $32.50; a hyena, $5; a cage of paroquets, $2.50; an Abyssinian boar, $35; and camels went from $20 to $47.50. The elephant, Betsy, was sold to Adam Forepaugh for $4,000. We learn from the trip route book that George Middleton was the on-the-lot manager as well as controlling the privileges. James Cooper did not accompany the show, but sent his son, J. E. Cooper, Jr. as doorkeeper to look after his interests. J. B. Gaylord was the general agent; Signor G. Agrati, the contracting agent; and J. Dodge, advertising agent. H. P. Lyons was the treasurer. James and Eugene Robinson, William Gorman, Pauline Lee, and animal man G. W. Johnson were the only performers from the summer tour retained for the trip. The number of ring performers listed totaled fifteen.

[8] King, Chapter 3, Part One, pp. 35-36.

[9] Detroit *Free Press,* June 5, 1879, p. 1.

[10] *Ibid.*

[11] Loeffler, "Candles, Flares, Gas, Electric, All Used to Light the Circus," p. 30. Advertising claims ran as high as a total of eighteen electric chandeliers in service. The Adam Forepaugh circus experimented with the use of electric illumination at the Detroit stand of July 5, 1879. Charles J. Vandepoele, a local electrician or "Detroit's Edison," introduced an original version of illumination. A single instrument was attached to one of the three center poles, the other two supporting the usual number of jets. The result was quite satisfactory, sufficient to induce manager Forepaugh into closing a contract with the inventor. Under its terms, Vandepoele was given six weeks to construct a new machine capable of illuminating both of the large pavilions in use. Forepaugh was to pay $7,000, furnish his own engine, and supply Vandepoele travel expenses for a week or two until someone could be properly trained to take charge of the lighting process.

[12] *Ibid.*

[13] Clipping, Chicago *Inter Ocean,* June 17, 1879, n.p.n.

[14] The usual program was arranged in the following order: (1) The grand entree by the entire company. (2) Caledonian sports, Crossley & Elder. (3) Military drill, pyramids, etc., the elephants. (4) Troupe of tumblers led by James Murray. (5) Principal equestrian act, William Dutton, with clown John Lowlow. (6) Feats of strength, Mme. D'Atalie. (7) Principal equestrian act, Frank Melville, with clown John Patterson. (8) Double trapeze, Lawrence Sisters. (9) Principal equestrienne act, Adelaide Cordona, with clown Joseph Kennebel. (10) Brother act, the Leotards. (11) Principal equestrian act, Charles Fish, with clown Peter Conklin. (12) Japanese juggling, Awati Katnochin. (13) Four-horse act, Adelaide Cordona. (14) *Battoute* leaping by the company, led by William Batcheller. The sideshow, managed by Edward C. Cole, included Myrtle Corbin, four-legged girl; C. B. Tripp, armless man; Eli Bowen, legless man; I. W. Sprague, living skeleton; Diobola, fire king; Mlle. Adeline, Circassian woman; Ashbury Benjamin, spotted boy; Zip, the What Is It?; Frank Morton, ventriloquist; Prof.

Padrienella's troupe of trained monkeys; Solomon Stone, light-ning calculator; Harry Roltair, magician; and Prof. E. J. Fry's Cornet Band. The concert was under the direction of Robert Butler. It consisted of Hall & Williams, clog dancers; La Belle Pauline, serio-comic songs; Miss Helene Smith, song and dance; Harry Roltair, acts of magic; M. McCullom, banjo solo; the Glue Brothers, acrobatic song and dance; O. Arbuckle, cannoneer; a *Humpty Dumpty* pantomime; and the whole ended with an act of firing a lady from a cannon.

[15] Clippings, Chicago *Inter Ocean,* June 19, 20, 1879, n.p.n.

[16] Baltimore *American and Commercial Advertiser,* April 24, 1879, p. 4.

[17] Hartford, CT, *Daily Courant,* May 20, 1880, p. 2.

[18] Clipping, St. Louis (MO) *Globe-Democrat,* May 29, 1880, n.p.n.

[19] *Ibid.*

[20] Barnum, *Struggles and Triumphs,* p. 740.

[21] Hamilton, St. Louis (MO) *Globe Democrat,* April 14, 1907, n.p.n.

EPILOGUE: MR. BAILEY AND MR. BARNUM

[1] New York *Clipper,* September 11, 1880, p. 195.

[2] New York *Clipper,* October 9, 1880, p. 227.

[3] New York *Clipper,* October 16, 1880, p. 235.

[4] New York *Clipper,* November 13, 1880, p. 267.

[5] New York *Clipper,* November 11, 1880, p. 287.

[6] New York *Clipper,* November 27, 1880, p. 288; December 25, p. 315. A stuffed hippopotamus went to the Pullman Bros. for $15; a stuffed lion to Mr. Kane for $30; to Mr. Cohen a stuffed giraffe for $6, a cage of stuffed birds for $15, and five female wax figures for $1; and an automatic cornet player to W. C. Coup for $8.

[7] New Haven (CT) *Sunday Union,* March 20, 1881, n.p.n.

[8] *Ibid.*

[9] Middleton, p. 42.

[10] Hamilton, St. Louis (MO) *Globe Democrat,* April 14, 1907, n.p.n.

BIBLIOGRAPHY

BOOKS

Barnum, P. T. (A. H. Saxon, editor). *Selected Letters of P. T. Barnum*. New York: Columbia University Press, 1982.

_____. *Struggles and Triumphs: or, The Life of P. T. Barnum*, Vol. II. New York: Alfred A. Knopf, 1927.

Coup, W. C. *Sawdust and Spangles*. Chicago: 1901.

Conklin, George, as told to Harvey W. Root. *The Ways of the Circus*. New York: Harper & Brothers, 1921.

Day, Charles H., [edited by William L. Slout]. *Ink From a Circus Press Agent*. San Bernardino (CA): The Borgo Press, 1995.

Frost, Thomas. *Circus Life and Circus Celebrities*. London: Chatto & Windus, 1881.

History of the Wonderful Baby Elephant, The. Author unknown. New York: New York Popular Publishing Company, 1880.

Howes, Jeanne Chretien. *The Howes Circus Story*. Weston, CT: self published, 1990.

Middleton, George (as told to and written by his wife). Self published, 1913.

Pember, A. *The Mysteries and Miseries of the Great Metropolis*. New York: D. Appleton and Company, 1874.

Sanger, Lord George. *Seventy Years a Showman*. New York: E. P. Dutton & Co., 1926.

Saxon, Arthur H. *P. T. Barnum: the Legend and the Man*. New York: Columbia University Press, 1989.

Thayer, Stuart. *Annals of the American Circus*, Vols. I, II, III. Self published, 1976-1992.

_____, and William L. Slout. *Grand Entrée: The Birth of the Greatest Show on Earth.* San Bernardino, CA: The Borgo Press, 1997.

_____. *Mudshows and Railers.* Ann Arbor (MI): self published, 1971.

PERIODICALS

Braathen, Sverre O. and Faye O., "Circus Monarchs," *Bandwagon*, March/April, 1970, pp. 4-8.

Carboy, John, "Bailey, Not Barnum!" clipping, New York *Dispatch*, April 19, 1891, n.p.n.

Clarke, Birkit, "Among the Showmen," New York *Clipper*, November 13, 1872, p. 324.

Cooke, Louis E., "Reminiscences of a Showman," Newark *Evening Star*, August 19, 1915, n.p.n.

Crosby, C. Fred, "The Early Days of Barnum's 'Greatest Show on Earth'," *Billboard*, January 21, 1922, pp. 49, 69.

Dahlinger, Fred, Jr., "The Development of the Railroad Circus," *Bandwagon,* January/February, pp. 28-36; March/April, pp. 28-36; May/June, 1884, 29-36, 1884.

Draper, John D., "The History of the Howes and the London Titles," *Bandwagon*, January/February, 1978, pp. 23-28.

_____, "Linda Jeal and Her Equestrian Kin," *Bandwagon,* May/June, 1987, p. 31.

Garvie, Billy G., "Old-Time Show Receipts," *Billboard*, March 21, 1914, p. 185.

Henderson, John M, "Winning Wealth and Wind," *Billboard*, September 7, 1907, pp. 17, 28.

King, Orin C., "Only Big Show Coming," Chapter 1, Part Two, *Bandwagon,* July/August, 1987, pp. 34-46; September/October, 1987, pp. 22-33; November/December, 1987, pp. 52-62; January/February, 1988, pp. 34-46.

Loeffler, Robert J. An analysis of newspaper reports to determine the actual number of cars in Barnum's 1872 train. *The White Tops,* May/June, 1983, pp. 35-43.

_____, "Candles, Flares, Gas, Electric, All Used to

Light the Circus," *The White Tops*, May/June, 1984, pp. 27-34.

_____, "A Re-Examination of the History of Madison Square Garden and the Role Played by the Ringlings in the History and Air Conditioning of the Garden," Part One, *Bandwagon*, March/April, 1973.

Mills, Pleasant J., "A Barnum Adv. Car Wreck," *The White Tops*, June, 1831, pp. 10-11.

"Monarch of Humbug," newspaper clipping, scrapbook SBK 17, Circus World Museum, n.d., n.p.n. It is unfortunate the reference in not more pricise.

"Nestor of Clowns, A," interview with Dan Castello, probably from the Syracuse *Standard*, n.d., n.p.n.

Shettel, James W., "She Knew Dan Rice," *The Circus Scrap Book*, January, 1930, pp. 29-41.

Sturtevant, C. G., "Getting It Up and Down," *Billboard*, March 24, 1928, p. 187.

_____, "Little Biographies of Famous American Circus Men," *The White Tops*, May, 1928, p. 5; August, 1928, p. 3; and January 1929, p. 6.

_____, "P. T. Barnum of Connecticut," *The White Tops*, May/June, 1934, n.p.n.

Thayer, Stuart, "Bad Press, Big Crowds: The Barnum Caravan of 1851-1854," *Bandwagon*, September/October, 1992, pp. 32-33.

_____, "Elephants for Barnum," *Bandwagon*, March/April 1990, pp. 30-31.

_____, "Joseph E. Warner: Pioneer of the Three Tent Circus," *Bandwagon*, January/February, 1970, pp. 20-23.

_____, "The Nathans, a Circus Family," *Bandwagon*, March/ April, 1985, pp. 24-28.

_____, "P. T. Barnum's Great Travelling Museum, Menagerie, Caravan and Hippodrome, the Season of 1871," *Bandwagon*, July/August, 1976, pp. 4-9.

_____, "P. T. Barnum's Great Travelling Museum, Menagerie, Caravan and Hippodrome, the Season of 1872," *Bandwagon*, September/October, 1990, pp. 21-24.

Werner, M. R., "The Triumphs of a Super-Showman," Part X, Chattanooga *Sunday Times*, September 16, 1923, n.p.n.

White, Charles H., "More Early Circus Memories," *Bandwagon*, August 15, 1944, p. 5.

Yadon, Gordon, "RBBB Actual Formation," *Banner Line*, May 15, 1970, pp. 7-10.

NEWSPAPERS

Albany (NY) *Argus*
Appleton (WI) *The Crescent*
Atlanta (GA) *Constitution*
Augusta (GA) *Chronicle and Sentinel*
Baltimore (MD) *American and Commercial Advertiser*
Battle Creek (MI) *Daily Journal*
Billboard
Boston (MA) *Daily Courier*
Boston (MA) *Globe*
Boston (MA) *Herald*
Boston (MA) *Post*
Buffalo (NY) *Commercial Advertiser*
Buffalo (NY) *Daily Courier*
Chattanooga (TN) *Sunday Times*
Chicago (IL) *Daily Tribune*
Chicago (IL) *Inter-Ocean*
Cincinnati (OH) *Commercial*
Cincinnati (OH) *Daily Gazette*
Cleveland (OH) *Herald*
Cleveland (OH) *Plain Dealer*
Clinton (IA) *The Clinton Age*
Decatur (IL) *Daily Republican*
Detroit (MI) *Free Press*
Evansville (IN) *Daily Journal*
Frank Leslie's Illustrated Weekly

Grand Rapids (WI) *Reporter*
Hartford (CT) *Daily Courant*
Jackson (MI) *Daily Citizen*
Janesville (WI) *City News*
Janesville (WI) *City Times*
Janesville (WI) *Daily Recorder*
Janesville (WI) *Gazette*
Kansas City (MO) *Journal of Commerce*
Kenosha (WI) *Telegraph*
LaCrosse (WI) *Republican and Leader*
Milwaukee (WI) *Commercial Times*
Milwaukee (WI) *Sentinel*
Monroe (WI) *Informer*
Monroe (WI) *Sentinel*
Newark (NJ) *Daily Advertiser*
New Haven (CT) *Sunday Union*
New York *Mercury*
New York (NY) *Times*
Ontario (Canada) *Reformer*
Oshkosh (WI) *Northwestern and Oshkosh Journal*
Philadelphia (PA) *Press*
Pittsburgh (PA) *Daily Union*
Pittsburgh (PA) *Post*
Providence (RI) *Daily Journal*
Richmond (VA) *Daily Dispatch*
Rochester (NY) *Evening Express*
Springfield (IL) *Sangamo Monitor*
St. John (New Brunswick) *Telegraph*
St. Joseph (MO) *Daily Morning Herald*
St. Louis (MO) *Globe-Democrat*
St. Louis (MO) *Post-Dispatch*
Syracuse (NY) *Standard*
Titusville (PA) *Morning Herald*
Toledo (OH) *Blade*
Toronto (Canada) *Daily Telegram*
Toronto (Canada) *Globe*

Troy (NY) *Daily Times*
Utica (NY) *Daily Observer*
Washington (DC) *Post*
Wilmington (DE) *Every Evening*

ROUTE BOOKS

P. T. Barnum's, 1872, 1873, 1876, 1877, 1879, 1880, 1881
Cooper, Bailey & Co., 1876, 1880
Adam Forepaugh's, 1878, 1880

MISCELLANEOUS

Dingess, John A. Unpublished observations of the circus world as
  he knew it, generally referred to as the Dingess Manuscript, a
  copy of which is in the Robert L. Parkinson Library and Research Center, Circus World Museum, Baraboo, WI. The
  handwritten original is in the Harry Hertzberg Circus Collection and Library, San Antonio, TX.
Newspaper clippings, Scrapbook SBK 17, Robert L. Parkinson
      Library and Research Center, Circus World Museum,
      Baraboo, WI.
New York *Clipper*, for the years covered in the text.
P. T. Barnum's Advance Couriers, 1871, 1872, 1873.
P. T. Barnum's Illustrated News, 1878.
Richard E. Conover notes, Robert L. Parkinson Library and Re-
  search Center, Circus World Museum, Baraboo, WI.

INDEX

www.ingramcontent.com/pod-product-compliance
Lightning Source LLC
Chambersburg PA
CBHW030918090426
42737CB00007B/240